MORAL PHILOSOPHY AND DEVELOPMENT

Tedros Kiros is a professor in the Department of Political Science, Boston University, Boston, Massachusetts 02215.

MORAL PHILOSOPHY AND DEVELOPMENT
The Human Condition in Africa

by

Tedros Kiros

Ohio University Center for International Studies
Monographs in International Studies

Africa Series Number 61
Athens, Ohio 1992

The books in the Center for International Studies Monograph
Series are printed on acid-free paper ∞

00 99 98 97 96 7 6 5 4 3

Library of Congress Cataloging-in-Publication Data

Kiros, Tedros, 1951–
    Moral philosophy and development : the human condition in
Africa / by Tedros Kiros
    p.   cm. – (Monographs in international studies. Africa
series; no. 61)
    ISBN 0-89680-171-3
    1. Africa–Economic conditions. 2. Africa–Dependency on
foreign countries. 3. Economics–History. 4. Economics–
Moral and ethical aspects.
    I. Title II. Series.
HC800.K57 1992   92-9546
338.96–dc20   CIP

To the memory of my father and the industrious and pious African peasants.

CONTENTS

ACKNOWLEDGEMENT

I particularly want to thank my editor, Prof. James Cobban at the Ohio University Press, for his competent and patient preparation of this book and also my friend and personal editor, Peggy Walsh of the University of Massachusetts, Boston.

I also want to thank all those persons who attended the African Studies Association meetings where I delivered the themes of this book; in particular Professor Tekle Wolde Michael for his competent responses to the arguments on development.

INTRODUCTION

This book is a product of several years' work, work that began in 1982 on the burning theme of the African food "crisis." Research and thinking on the theme of the African food crisis in due course impelled me to delve deeper into the genesis and archeology of the elusive concept of "development," which culminated in writing a piece in 1984 on the subject of the causes (historical/moral) of Africa's sustained history of material underdevelopment. The fruits of that research encouraged me to seek a theoretical attempt at the possible resolution of the food crisis in particular and the general state of material backwardness that characterizes the fifty-five or so modern African states. The painful awareness of the material aspect of the human condition in Africa led me to return to the study of classical political economy and the types of moral imperatives upon which this political economy was grounded. From the study of classical political economy, I attempted to draw a judicious interpretation of the type of development models that were specifically applied to deal with the human condition in Africa, models that are amply demonstrated by the historical legacies of slavery and colonialism, and the development packages of the 1960s.

A judicious reading of classical political economy, I argue, uncovers tensions between certain implicit moral concerns and explicit economic imperatives (profit motive, cost-benefit, utility, and efficiency, for example). I am of the opinion that the study of classical political economy, and the tensions (as opposed to the existence of a solid doctrine) between the moral and economic dimensions that I seek to unfold is a novel way of looking at (a) why Africa failed to develop a self-sustaining mode of production in its historical confrontations with slavery and colonialism, and (b) how Africa now can attempt to materially develop itself as an integral part of an aggressive world economy, and effectively energize dormant resources in contemporary Africa, particularly in the areas affected by the food crisis. The central themes of this book then are the logically and historically interpenetrating ones of food, the reality of underdevelopment, and the possibility of a well-rounded development. I shall elaborate on the following themes: in chapter 1, food, ideology, and hegemony; in chapter 2, the meanings and causes of material underdevelopment; in chapters 3 and 4, the possibilities of well-rounded development; and in chapter 5, the notion of thinking as a moral activity.

A careful and empirically well-grounded student of African history who wants to responsibly assess the African present must begin with the study of slavery, colonialism, imperialism, and in particular and perhaps even more important the role of racism. In short, the histories of the legacies of slavery, colonialism, imperialism, and racism ought to command the present normative gaze of any student who purports to answer the question, Why is Africa (except for relatively minor flashes of material development in Kenya, Ivory Coast, Zimbabwe, South Africa, and parts of Nigeria) still underdeveloped? There is a sense in which the above methodology is valid, as the respected contributions of Fanon, Cabral, Rodney, and the early Nkrumah attest.[1] Their contributions have in several ways provided an adequate response to some of the conventional observations that came from a historical study of the African past. There is, however, another sense in which the various contributions of Fanon, Cabral, Rodney, and Nkrumah, to name just a few, do not adequately meet the challenging thesis of those students of the African past who in subtle ways attempt to impute the facts of African underdevelopment not to external factors such as slavery, colonialism, imperialism, and racism but to internal factors: the inadequacies of the African self image, the African view of external nature, the African unproductive class, and Africa's indigenously developed, albeit highly rudimentary technology (as in ancient Abyssinia). The themes of this book then enter the ongoing conversations and debates about the African past and the present.

---

[1]See Frantz Fanon, *The Wretched of the Earth* (New York: Grove Press, 1968), Emilcar Cabral, *Return to the Source* (New York: Monthly Press, 1973), Walter Rodney, *How Europe Underdeveloped Africa* (Washington D.C.: Howard University, 1971), and Kwame Nkrumah, *Neo-Colonialism* (New York: International Publishers, 1971).

The contributions that I attempt to make are intended to be positive responses to the doubts of those Africanists who might believe that Africans are incapable of materially developing the continent, and a caveat to those Africanists who uncritically expect Africa to develop materially as soon as all those external factors are eliminated and who are, relatively speaking, silent about those internal factors that have fully penetrated the African present and have almost become its second nature. I attempt to analyze critically the concerns, presuppositions and one-sided orientations of looking at the African past and present. It is a difficult, if not impossible, position in which to be; nevertheless, I do try to mediate between the two and come up with what I hope will be accepted as a novel proposition that neither idealizes the African conception of the self and of external nature, nor unduly and insensitively places the heavy burden of material backwardness upon the shoulders of Africans themselves—be it the African "elite" or the primordially "uninventive," "unimaginative," "unproductive," and backward-looking African peasantry. Against the dogmas of the above schools of thought—to the extent that I am capable, since I am also penetrated by prejudices, presuppositions, and subjective intellectual tastes—I seek to advance a proposition that looks at the African past and present with sensitivity and knowledge.

This book does not begin with a review of the massive literature about African history in order to reflect on the contemporary human condition in Africa; historical awareness, of course, is crucial in that the knowledge of the past enables us to better understand the present. Mistakes often can be prevented from repeating themselves if we somehow master the past so as to prevent similar errors from penetrating the present and thus causing history to repeat itself. Certain forms of repetition such as slavery, colonialism, dependencies of any kind can serve as instructive historical lessons provided that historians return to history, not because they are expected professionally to do so, but because history—the history of human beings, their joys, sufferings, pains, and mistakes—expects a grand task from them. History looks at us with the eyes, ears, and voices of the present.

My attempt at thinking about the abstract concept of material underdevelopment and the proliferation of writings that that concept has rightly made possible begins with an observation on the contemporary human condition in Africa: the shocking sight of the ashamed and frightened bodies of the African poor that the food "crisis" has magnified from the almost invisible existence of poverty on that continent. It was my decision to observe the human condition in Africa as if it were directly my problem, as if the continent-wide food crisis were my own crisis, which imperceptibly led me to study Africa and to set my professional training in philosophy and political science to work. In this way, the book begins not with a discussion of African history, particularly African economic history, as the logic would dictate, but rather with a discussion of the absence of food, the absolutely necessary human need—the need around which "civilization" in its spiritual and material form might one day be formed. The first few questions with which I attempt to deal, as in the first chapter below, are as follows: Why is there a food crisis in Africa? Should there be a food crisis at all? The proposition that I advance in reflecting on these questions is elaborated in detail in the first chapter. I will now highlight some of the main ideas.

Ideally, people might come to think of food as an inalienable right to which all human beings should be entitled. Rarely, however, are individuals encouraged to think about food that way. Instead, people conceive of food as a commodity, a good, an object that one has to work for and obtain, either directly in one's own backyard, as in all precapitalistic forms of society such as Africa's precolonial past, or in more organized forms from factories via a chain of food stores. In either case, food is obtained either directly by the food producer, without surpluses that are worth bringing to the market; or indirectly by working at places outside one's immediate land, and obtaining the money to buy food as a commodity, a good, an object. In the second form of obtaining food, a form dominant in the twentieth century, and in which a well-organized market is the medium through which food is exchanged, food begins to lose its human value as an nonalienable right, and becomes a market commodity, obtainable with money. Food is produced, circulated, exchanged, and consumed as a commodity, a good, an object, just like any other commodity. In the market mentality, the distinctively human quality of food is forgotten. It is imperative, I will argue, that the market mentality infuses itself with some pragmatically effective moral/rational principles.

There was a period in the history of Africa prior to to its penetration by colonialism and by the global world economy during which African food producers circulated and consumed food among themselves. I contend that the preslavery and precolonial Africa was less marked than the present by the dominant market form that sustained itself systematically through the subtle yet powerful, invisible yet diffuse, hidden yet violent power of hegemonic ideology. By ideology, I understand the power of ideas—ideas that gently govern, direct, guide men's and women's consciousnesses and states of mind. This particular understanding of governance, self-governance which may be grounded upon the material infrastructure of a society, is identified here as hegemonic. The tendency to look at food as a commodity, accessible only to those who have the means to buy food, thereby securing an everyday existence, and to look at those who fail to have the means as predestined victims of poverty, famines, starvation, and malnutrition, has become almost second nature in the modern age. This tendency, I argue in chapter 1, is the unconscious effect of ideology—or ideas that I call hegemonic ideas. I further attempt concretely to show the way these ideas insinuate themselves into our lives—through preachings and sermons in churches, journal articles, clubs, schools, and through many other professional institutions of our lives in a civil society. Ideas also are disseminated through some of the concrete institutions of the state as the new Leviathan, that is, through the courts, the legislature, and the police. I identify the institutions of civil society and the state as *hegemonic apparatuses*. The ways in which the food crisis originated in the African context are discussed within the framework of hegemonic ideas and hegemonic apparatuses. An effort is also made to explore some possibilities of overcoming the problems rooted in hegemonic ideas through what I call a *counterhegemonic* vision, a vision that may give us an alternative conception of development and progress. I introduce the notion in chapter 1 and discuss it in great detail in chapters 3, 4, and 5.

I now turn to make some general remarks on chapter 2. The themes of chapter 1 inevitably contribute to the raising of several questions about the perennial problems associated with the concept of material underdevelopment. Two questions in particular immediately come to one's mind: first, why is it that the modes of production which Africa once had during the preslavery and colonial epochs and in which basic foodstuffs were available to the primary producers did not leave lasting and self-sustaining economic institutions? and second, what is distinctive about the African concepts of the self, of external nature, and of the technology of transforming nature, that may account for Africa's material underdevelopment? I attempt to answer these two questions by a method of inquiry which I call *constructive refutation*; I employ this method to review the massive literature of three schools of thought: the political-social-cultural school, the dependency school, and the political economy school. I read the literature appropriating the insights that seemed worth retaining and criticizing those that merited criticism. In the end, I will attempt to synthesize the notion of hegemonic ideas with the useful insights of the literature by distilling from the literature of the various schools of thought those ideas that I think significantly illuminate how Africans themselves can be reunderstood through their ideas of the self, particularly the moral self, and of external nature, and through the types of science and technologies that they did and did not develop. I especially stress, as I did in the first chapter, the powerful role that ideas played prior to the penetration of slavery and colonialism, and I advance the proposition that it is a sensitive understanding of that period of African history that is the pivot to the understanding of the African present.

I think that this proposition is a novel way of assessing the meaning of material underdevelopment in the African context. I must warn my readers that the concept of self in Africa is not intended to present Africans as human beings who collectively possess a distinctive psyche. For me, Africans are part and parcel of humankind; there is nothing distinctive about them except their collectively shared attempts (with the exception of the well-to-do African elites and privileged farmers) to develop rudimentary technologies so as to transform nature within the constraints of revering nature. From the transformation of nature, Africans might develop a nonalienated view of nature similar to the romantic views of nature which others might have practiced prior to the consolidation of a global world economy oriented toward the insensitive domination of nature by science. The concept of nature as subject to development through domination by science and technology and the view of nature as our other are themes that I also discuss in great detail in chapter 3. I also introduce the idea of the possible existence of a nondominating view of nature as an integral dimension of the African or, if you will, the precapitalist view of world cultures in chapter 2. I again return to this theme through the Husserlian notion of the life-world as applied to the African view of nature in chapter 4.

Chapters 3 and 4 are attempts at making a novel contribution to moral philosophy and political economy by (1) making an original appropriation of classical political economy, particularly the moral and political economies of Adam Smith's chief works *The Theory of Moral Sentiments* and *The Wealth of Nations*, then (2) proceeding to draw new insights that may fruitfully inform the models of economic development relevant to Africa, (3) appropriating John Rawls' famous *Theory of Justice*, and finally (4) providing a highly personal attempt to develop some basic but self-generated principles of justice that I hope will guide the programs and visions of the notions of well-rounded development in Africa. For the rest of this introduction, I will briefly remark on the four points above.

Regarding (1) above, in the appropriation of Smith's chief works, there is a tension in Adam Smith's seemingly irreconcilable commitments to the demands of a strict political economy and the demands of a socially sensitive and rigorous moral philosophy. There are gaps, empty spaces, incomplete thoughts, discontinuities, and even inconsistencies between the theories of *The Theory of Moral Sentiments* and the world famous *The Wealth of Nations*. Textual analysis of the tensions has led me to conclude that, for Smith, political economy does not reflect its *fundamental obligation* (in my view) to deal with the exploitation of man by man insofar as the quest for capital accumulation and profit extraction render exploitation an imperative. I propose that Smith's implicit moral sentiments in human beings would not refuse to control "some of the selfish passions" when those selfish passions tempt human beings to do things that are reprehensible from a rational-moral point of view. Thus, political economy can contribute to the founding of an efficient and stable economic system if, and only if, the social passions regulate, guide, and constructively "discipline" the unsocial and the selfish passions. In this way, I argue, the themes of *The Theory of Moral Sentiments* may be reconciled with the theses of *The Wealth of Nations*.

I now move on to (2) above and draw from my melding of Smith's philosophies some applications to the theme of Africa's material underdevelopment. At issue here is the question "How can and how should Africa become materially developed?" A possible answer to this question requires a reevaluation of the models of economic development that Africa inherited from the colonial past as well as the so-called "socialist" models that Africa uncritically accepted during the postcolonial period. Both models, as contemporary African economic reality attests, have led to disaster: to mention just one glaring example, the food crisis. The challenge of the 1980's for Africa as a whole was to seek immediate solutions to the following three urgent problems. First is the need to develop less nationalistic but more continent-oriented "leaders" in all spheres of African life: statesmen, educators, advisors, and scientific thinkers. Second is the need to found new educational institutions that are capable of creatively developing Africa's dormant material resources and existing traditional values and practices such as attitudes toward health and child-rearing, traditional public moralities, and the old theories and practices of farming. In short, Africans themselves, as do Europeans and Asians, need to look at the remnants of their existing tradition both reverentially and critically so as to transform contemporary Africa and become respected members of the modern world. The African farmers in particular must be given a chance to initiate a new beginning. African traditions, in their potentially transformable form, may thus prove to be particularly enriching to human heritage. The challenge is there; Africans must recognize that challenge and convert it into a visible reality. The human condition in Africa in the 1980's then promises numerous possibilities rather than impossibilities. There is hope for the rational African will to transform the continent if Africans seize the opportunity, act responsibly, and cease to despair.

Third, there is a need now somehow to acknowledge the merits of market and planned economies, as the Chinese have done, so as to make material development possible and then move on in the foreseeable future to develop—with the help of some of the morally progressive remnants of Africa's value systems—an *authentic ethical community* as part and parcel of a possible *authentic ethical world community*. The relevant point is that African developers must learn how to work skillfully with existing capitalism without abandoning the quest for an authentic ethical community. The food crisis in Africa can no longer be solved by worn-out Marxist-Leninist dogmas of a "planned economy" but rather by a fresh and independent reunderstanding of a socially, economically, and politically, democratic "free enterprise" system. Africa, as successful economic countries in Asia (Japan, Taiwan, South Korea, and Singapore), must use capitalism with the intention of constructing an authentic ethical community in contemporary Africa. The capitalist spirit must first be experienced before it is rejected.

In chapter 5, I will argue that Rawls' truly admirable attempt to contribute toward the resolution of deep inequalities within the democratic "regimes" of the West by provoking us to think about justice (on the plane of morality as well as on the plane of politics) can and should be extended to the African human condition as well. In chapter 1, I only mention the importance and relevance of Rawls' *A Theory of Justice*; in chapter 5 I return to his significant ideas.

Rawls rightly notes the importance of formulating some potentially universal principles of justice, principles which are sufficiently comprehensive and reasonable that rational and moral human beings would be willing to assess them and possibly use them as guides in their lives. This part of the scope of justice is both sufficiently abstract and politically useful that it may serve as an ideal way of regulating the perennial problems of justice in human affairs. However, for Rawls, the two principles of justice that he originated are principles that grew from the particular historical experience of the West; specifically these principles are meant to address the deep inequalities (racial, economic, social, political, and psychological) as they exist in American democracy. Rawls then develops a theory of justice that specifically attempts to contribute toward a politically reasonable way of dealing with problems of justice in the West, with a particular focus on the United States. His concept of justice is regional. In spite of its regionality, however, with some amplification his conception of justice could deal with Africa.

On the other hand, I argue, as did the philosophers Plato and Kant, that to think about justice is to think about what the human self is capable of doing when it is guided by the passion for truth, a passion that by definition is of universal concern. Thus, a theory of justice can be developed in such a way that all thoughtful human beings can submit to it, not for the sake of grasping knowledge, but for the sake of thinking about the ideal and lofty possibilities it opens. This is how I have interpreted the project of Rawls, in spite of his explicit warnings that his theory of justice is a contribution to the immediate concerns of democratic regimes in general and the American regime in particular.

I also claim that some of the features of the principles of justice, particularly those legacies of colonialism which began in Europe and gradually entered America, cut across the history of at least three continents: South America, Africa, and Europe. Consequently, the historical interaction among the races of humankind in these three continents clearly makes application of the principles of justice universal rather than particular. Since this book is about the human condition in Africa, and since the condition of humanity in Africa is influenced by the legacies of colonialism, and since those legacies grew from the interaction of Europeans and Africans, it follows that the two principles of justice that Rawls has concisely formulated could be amplified and then relevantly appropriated to guide the discussion of deep inequalities that obtain in African countries as well. The food crisis can be handled adequately by a careful application of the two principles of justice which I have put forward.

Before I move on to the first chapter though, I need to give a justification of the specific theories of development with which I shall work. The authors who have contributed to the discussion of why Africa is still undeveloped and hopelessly haunted by hunger are numerous. After ten years of a careful study of political economy and moral philosophy, however, I am convinced that a deep understanding of the African present from a synchronic point of view must be carefully guided by a diachronic historical sensibility. The miserable African present is conditioned (not determined) by the ideas of development that directly grew out of classical political economy and which gradually infused the various packages of development with which governments experimented in Africa from the 1960s to the 1980s as exemplified in the World Bank's vision of developing Africa.

For the sake of simplicity I attempt to frame my thesis that ideologies have affected the models of development which African policy leaders in particular have followed within four categories under which I subsume various schools of thought that have attempted to understand the African mind. The various scholars that I cite within the scope of the categories were chosen for the following reasons:

1. Their theories of development are bold, controversial, often lucid, and ideologically explicit
2. The themes of their works are perennial, for example, the question of Africa's "primitive," "stagnant," and "inferior" culture
3. The notion of "dependency," though dogmatic, is still engaging, a stimulant to thought
4. The tensions between "bourgeois" amoral economics and a subtly morally sensitive economic thinking in Adam Smith has deep reverberations on the human condition in Africa
5. Luxury items are being produced at the expense of the neglect of agriculture, from which arose what Sarah Berry has called the "agrarian crisis." Contemporary historians, economists, and political scientists have boldly and honestly criticized the corruptive role of luxury items, items that are produced specifically for the urban sector (the leaders, the bureaucrats, the highly ostentatious privileged consumers, and the "delicate" professionals)

The above five reasons are my justifications for choosing the literature that runs through this book, namely (1) classical political economy along with Marx's critical confrontations, (2) the cultural school, particularly Weber and McClelland's works, (3) the school of dependency, and (4) my own innovations of hegemonic theories.

HEGEMONIC AND COUNTERHEGEMONIC VISION

This chapter develops a theory from the idea of hegemony for an analysis of the African food crisis. The theory will then be applied toward an analysis of the following questions:

1. What is the meaning of the concept of hegemony and how could it be applied in the analysis of the African food crisis?
2. Is the African food crisis a natural one and therefore unsolvable except, perhaps, through redemption, or is it resolvable by human efforts?
3. To what extent is the food crisis affected and conditioned by ideology, and what is the nature of that ideology?
4. Should food be a pawn of ideology?
5. How could Africans help themselves, and what can people do, particularly the intellectuals, to contribute toward the alleviation of the food crisis?

The structure of the argument is as follows. The first part gives an exposition of the concept of hegemony and theorizes about the possibility of applying it in the analysis of the food crisis. The second part reviews the literature and examines the relationship between ideology and the food crisis. The third part discusses the scope of the food crisis and introduces the idea of counterhegemonic vision. A special attempt is made to free the discussion from ideology so that we can revitalize the human dimension of the food crisis. This part ends with a suggestion of what Africans themselves can do to assuage the food crisis in concert with help from the world community. The fourth part contends that the food crisis in Africa is also a moral problem that may be solved by all members of human society. The concluding remarks of the fifth part make some tentative proposals toward solutions of the African food crisis from the angle of what we call the counterhegemonic vision.

The Concepts of Hegemony and Ideology

The question to be addressed here again is "What is the meaning of the concept of hegemony and how could it be applied in the analysis of the food crisis?" The concept of hegemony has recently commanded an impressive array of attention from a wide range of thinkers in political philosophy and sociology.[1]

At the outset, it should be noted that scholars disagree on the meaning of hegemony. Given its rich ambiguity, it has generated an equally rich proliferation of perspectives. Some contend that hegemony is a particular type of leadership that is based not primarily on the use of violence or coercion, but on the systematic spread of the world view of the ruling class.[2] We shall

---

[1]The literature on hegemony is extensive. For discussions see the following: Joseph Femia, "Hegemony and Consciousness in the Thought of Antonio Gramsci," *Political Studies* 23 (1975): 8-32; Thomas Bates, "Gramsci and the Theory of Hegemony," *Journal of the History of Ideas* 36 (1975): 351-61; Walter Adamson, *Hegemony and Revolution: Antonio Gramsci's Political and Cultural Theory* (California: University of California Press, 1980); L. Salamini, "Gramsci and Marxist Sociology of Knowledge: An Analysis of Hegemony-Ideology-Knowledge," *Sociological Quarterly* 15 (1974): 359-80; C. Mouffe, ed., *Gramsci and Marxist Theory* (London: Routledge and Kegan Paul, 1979); and Tedros Kiros, *Toward the Construction of a Theory of Political Action; Antonio Gramsci* (New York: University Press of America, 1985). There is an extensive bibliography in the last that includes all the major discussions of hegemony.

[2]For Bates, it is through the activity of the intellectuals that hegemony gains a concrete political form. As he puts it, "The intellectuals succeed in creating hegemony to the extent that they extend the world view of the rulers to the ruled, and thereby secure the free consent of the masses to the law and order of the land. To the extent that the intellectuals fail to create hegemony, the ruling class falls back on the State's coercive apparatus." See Bates, "Gramsci and the Theory of Hegemony," 353. For Mouffe, on the other hand, hegemony is not just the imposition of the dominant ideology—that is, the ideology

call this an instrumentalist conception of hegemony in which by instrumentalist we understand the use of a particular idea as a means to attain a particular end. According to this view, a set of ideas is diffused into what Gramsci calls civil society and political society as a means by which the members of civil society and political society are subtly taught to think and behave in certain ways. Civil society is composed of schools, churches, clubs, journals, and political parties. Political society is composed of public institutions such as government, courts, police, and the army; in these institutions, unlike those of civil society, the members are made to behave in certain acceptable ways by the means of direct domination and when necessary by the use of force by the State. In civil society, a set of ideas is used to achieve one coherent end—consent combined with conformity. In political society, this end is achieved not through the spread of ideas but through the threat of use of force, not through the use of speech and persuasion but through violence.

Hegemony then has two aspects: consent achieved by education, and violence. The aspect of consent is usually the part of hegemony that is dominant in the twentieth century; the second aspect, violence, is always available for use during times of desperation. It is resorted to when members of civil society dissent, revolt, and refuse to be governed. It is a means of suppression.

For us, it is the first aspect of hegemony (through education) that is relevant to the analysis of the food crisis in Africa. We will thus start with the discussion of this aspect from a different angle before we proceed to apply it to Africa.

Gramsci's conception of hegemony grew out of his engaging confrontation with Marx's views of ideology. To put the matter in perspective, consider the following statement by Marx:

---

of the ruling class upon the dominated classes—rather, it is a subtly exercised form of transforming the belief systems of the dominated classes so that they complement the dominant world view of those in power or those who are coming to power. This form consists in "a process of transformation (aimed at producing) a new form and of rearticulation of existing ideological elements." See Mouffe, *Gramsci and Marxist Theory*, 192.

3

the distinction should always be made between the material transformation of the economic conditions of production . . . and the legal, political, religious, aesthetic, or philosophic . . . in short, ideological forms in which men become conscious of this conflict and fight it out.[3]

Here it seems that for Marx law, politics, religion are nothing but the ideological, therefore false and distorted, forms of men's life because they reflect the one-sided, exploitative, and dehumanizing views held by the ruling class. Furthermore, he claims that these ideological forms tend to mystify reality, instead of disclosing, revealing, and illuminating it. By so arguing, Marx assumes that through the activity of mystification, ideology hides reality from the reflective and rational power of historical explanation. In particular, Marx asserts, ideology mystifies the real working of the economy, the material conditions of life. To expose this mystification, Marx engaged in the critique of economic ideologies. That is as far as Marx went.

At this point, Gramsci joins the discussion with his novel concept of hegemony. Gramsci argues that granted, ideology does often mystify reality, but that is not all it does. Gramsci agrees with Marx that ideology, by mystifying reality, indirectly serves the interests of the ruling class in that it causes the ruled to accept passively their material conditions replete with food shortages, poverty, or diseases. For example, a distorted and irrational interpretation of religion serves as an ideological veil behind which secular problems are hidden and are rationalized as transcendental aspects of the human condition. Given such an ideological veil of mystification, the ruling class rules without any resistance. But then Gramsci supplements Marx in a fundamental and original sense that there is a way by which ideology demystifies reality. He argues that the ideological forms—religion, politics, philosophy, and so forth—in fact are not false, nor are they merely expressions of the economy; they actually are crystallizations of the contradictions of life itself. Simply put, they are ideas and visions that are not yet

---

[3]Karl Marx, *A Contribution to the Critique of Political Economy* (New York: International Library, 1903), 12.

wholes; they are inadequate expressions of the ideals of men and women given the stage of their human consciousness. They are visions that are anxiously yearning for concrete realization. They are the very content of the "not-yet."

Ideology then, says Gramsci, essentially exposes the contradictions of the economy; it brings the contradictions to the forefront for everybody to experience, but without the crucial component of how to resolve them. Instead of offering solutions, ideologies serve the purpose of teaching the ruled to accept these contradictions as final. This false sense of finality, however, shows at least two things: (1) the human subjects have internalized certain unexplained, unreflected-upon ideas from their continuous exposure to the institutions of civil society; and (2) when life's contradictions come to the center of everyday experience, and the human subjects attempt to resist blind acceptance of those contradictions, political society, fearful of losing its legitimacy, threatens its subjects with the use of force. More often than not, the ruled respond with only silence and political passivity.

The counterhegemonic project here is the continuous effort to stimulate the human subject to question critically, examine, and intellectually overthrow the effects of ideologies that have generated those distorted and false religions, political ideas, and philosophies. This theme will be discussed further in chapters 2 and 3.

Ideology, according to Gramsci, can demystify reality to the precise extent that it unfolds the contradictory constitution of warring ideologies, opening the possibility of reconciling reality with conflicting ideologies as a task to be carried out by the enlightened and conscious members of a given community. It is to this version of the function of ideology that the concept of hegemony is a path-breaking addition.

We are now in a position to state as precisely as possible what hegemony means for Gramsci. The basic idea is that an understanding of human experience requires an understanding of the indispensable role, function, and contribution of material and nonmaterial forces: for example, money or religious ideas. Human experience is in fact an embodiment of ideas—religious, philosophic, political, and aesthetic. Human beings may begin to think critically. They may come to the realization that life will never be paradise but it does not follow that life should be miserable. This critical realization enables human beings to conceive of themselves as moral and rational agents who can transform ideas into new possibilities for leading their lives. Ideas in the hands of critical human beings are the foundations of human action. We now add emphatically as we did earlier that ideas become public policies and are made visible to the masses through the mediational role of intellectuals. The intellectuals carry these ideas to civil society as teachers, preachers, editors, party leaders, advisors, and politicians. Ideas are disseminated simply through books, public lectures, and, most prominent of all, through the effects of public policy.

The concept of hegemony is useful in the understanding of the food crisis in Africa. The crisis in Africa, we argue, to a significant extent is conditioned by the infiltration of certain hegemonic ideas—economic, political, religious, and philosophical. These ideas are international as well as national. They are international in the sense that the food crisis has links with the international production of the other commodities for which food is exchanged. Also, during times of crisis, food is often transported to the crisis areas from countries that have it in excess. Some of these countries use the crisis to dump their excess; and other countries contribute out of a sense of moral obligation, a reflection of ideas that are grounded in a deeply internalized set of ethical and philosophical values. Still other members of the international community, on the other hand, do not seem to care to offer help; such members often adhere to ideas that deemphasize the ethical dimension of the food crisis.

Food, Ideology, and Hegemonic Apparatuses

For the convenience of our readers, we shall restate the questions which will be analyzed here:

1. Is the African food crisis a natural one, therefore unsolvable except perhaps through redemption, or is it an artificial problem brought about by human beings and therefore resolvable by human efforts?
2. To what extent is the food crisis affected and conditioned by ideology as defined by Gramsci?

6

We would deal with these questions by firstly reviewing the relevant literature which pertains to the food crisis and then by contrasting our evaluation of the literature with what we call the counterhegemonic vision. As Hopkins and Puchala put it,

> As social scientists, we begin from the assumption that food systems are social systems as much as they are biological ones, and food problems are political and institutional as much as agricultural. Food production, distribution and consumption are purposeful acts; following implicitly or explicitly from calculated decisions within the context of formal and informal institutions.[4]

This statement is a partly accurate characterization of the nature of food as that basic necessity without which human beings cannot maintain their humanity, provided that a well thought out system of agriculture under astute and morally unimpeachable persons is readily available. The unavailability of such a system is largely responsible for the food crisis.

In Africa, there is a food crisis of alarming magnitude. The term crisis is itself alarming. In what sense then can we talk about crisis? By crisis, following Habermas, we understand the occurrence of a phenomenon within a given structure of a social and political system in which there are "fewer possibilities for problem solving than are necessary to the continued existence of the system. In this sense, crises are seen as persistent disturbances of system integration."[5] Habermas contends further that "crises in social systems are not produced through accidental changes in the environment, but through structurally inherent system imperatives that are incompatible and cannot be hierarchically integrated."[6]

---

[4]Raymond F. Hopkins and Donald J. Puchala, *The Global Political Economy of Food* 32/3 (Summer 1978).

[5]Jurgen Habermas, *The Legitimation Crisis* (Boston: Beacon Press, 1969), 2.

[6]Habermas, *Legitimation Crisis*, 4.

In Africa today, there is a crisis in this social scientific sense, but that is not all; the social scientific meaning of crisis is a rather abstract conceptualization of crises which is quite helpful, but not complete. It rightly points out that given certain inadequate structures, crisis inevitably follows. What are those structures? An analytic way of identifying these structures is provided by Marx in his seminal work: *Capital*. For Marx, the structures are those that belong to market economies.

Marx understands that the possibility for crisis lies "solely in the separation of sale from purchase."[7] An elementary example of this would be the contrast between a demand for food, as in Africa, and a lack of purchasing power; therefore, what is available for sale does not have a corresponding demand.[8] Demand and supply thus become separated. When this is the case, crisis may be the result. This is one meaning of crisis; there is a second one, however, which Marx describes as operating on the global level, and which we contend has an effect on the African food market. The second form is a direct consequence of money being transformed into an indispensable "means of payment."[9] The dogmatic view of money founded upon capitalistic ideas is

---

[7]Robert Tucker, *Marx and Engels Reader*, 2nd ed. (New York: W.W. Norton, 1978), 45.

[8]Lynn Scarlet, "Tropical Africa: Food or Famine," in *Food Politics: Regional Conflict*, by David N. Ballam and Michael J. Carey (Totowa, N.J.: Allanhead Osmun, 1981). Scarlet contends that indeed there is a growing demand for food in Africa, which contributes to the crisis. A typical crisis occurs in that the consumers in the city do not have the money with which to pay for the food at a socially desirable price. From the consumer's perspective, this is because the various commodities that are produced in the city are not selling at all; that is to say, there is no money. If there was enough money, the produce of the peasant would be bought at the desired price. From the perspective of the peasant, this can lead to various actions; he will either starve to death if he does not sell or if he sells at a very low price without profit at all; consequently, he will not produce enough to sell beyond what he needs to sustain himself or herself. When this happens, "crisis" occurs—crisis of "money as payment."

[9]Tucker, *Max and Engels Reader*, 456.

8

unwilling to consider bartering as a logical way with which human beings can alleviate immediate hunger. Money need not be the only instrument with which human beings can feed themselves; an equivalent exchange of what they have for what they do not have may do the job. Again, I will illustrate with a simple example. In a given African state, where there is agricultural production in the country and where there are sales markets in the cities, a typical crisis occurs when there is a great demand for food in the city, but there is no corresponding money with which consumers could buy food. Money is not available and, without it, payments of any sort cannot take place. As to crisis on the level of the production process, it will be touched upon later in the discussion of food as a commodity as an economic idea that governs the production, distribution, exchange, and consumption of food in Africa.

Above, we have identified two meanings of crisis—the social scientific one and the economic one. The two together constitute the ultimate meaning of crisis. We can now say that given these meanings, there is a crisis of food in Africa in that (1) there is an artificial shortage of food in spite of the demand of the starving human subjects; (2) there is lack of money with which the food can be bought; and (3) there are no easy ways of overcoming these problems stated in (1) and (2) above without introducing new structures as replacements for the prevailing structures of market economy. These new structures may be called authentically planned economies. Obviously, this is a rather ambitious demand, consistent with the demand for the counterhegemonic ideas that would serve as the foundations of potential structures. This is a task that needs to be demanded of the rulers by the primary producers and consumers in Africa and by the direct initiative of the peasants, the producers of food.

The African food crisis is of course directly affected by the food situation on the global level. Scholars are convinced that on the global level, the complexity of the food situation requires the participation of various disciplines.[10] The food situation on the global level is currently characterized by scarcity of resources—

---

[10]Lester Brown has called for such efforts. See Lester Brown and Arta Azis, eds., *Hunger, Politics and Markets* (New York: New York University Press, 1975).

9

scarcity of water, energy, and fertilizers.[11] Lester Brown has identified soil erosion as one of the chief factors that has contributed to a prolonged existence of poverty on a global scale.[12] As Brown commented,

> If soils continue to deteriorate in Africa, the decade-long decline in food output per person there could become chronic, leading to an ever-widening crisis. If excessive soil erosion and the other forces that slowed growth for the world as a whole continue to intensify, and if the projected increases in population materialize, then growth in food production could fall below that of population for the world as a whole during the 1980s.[13]

Obviously, there are some fundamental implications on the global plane for the food situation in Africa. After all, African food markets are integral aspects, albeit as unequals, of the world food market. Africans used to not only produce what is sufficient for themselves but also export some crucial cash crops to the rest of the world. They are exporters of Ghanaian cocoa, West African palm oils, East African coffee, Kenyan tea and pyrenthrum, as well as cotton from the Sudan, Egypt, and Uganda. As producers and exporters of these cash crops the shortages of water, energy, and fertilizers and the recorded problem of soil erosion on the global level *mutatis mutandis* severely vitiates the efforts of the peasant growers to feed themselves.

---

[11]Brown and Azis, *Hunger*, 11.

[12]Brown and Azis, *Hunger*, 12.

[13]Lester Brown, "Soils and Civilization," *Third World Quarterly* 5/1 (January 1983): 118. See also Philip H. Abelson, *Food: Politics, Economics, Nutrition and Research* (Washington: American Association for the Advancement of Science, 1975).

The magnitude of the food crisis in Africa was reported in the *New York Times*.[14] Yet Africa continues to be a continent of hope as well as despair; hope because a number of studies staunchly support the view that tropical Africa possesses vast potential for increasing its food production,[15] and because Africa as a whole is well endowed with land in relation to its population, "containing nearly 23 percent of the world's land area, about 14 percent of its agricultural area, and with only about 10 percent of the world's population."[16] It is a continent in despair in that it continues to be affected by droughts, famines, chronic poverty, and disease.[17] The question is why? In what follows, we will attempt to address this question in several stages. Before we provide our insights from the angle of hegemony, however, we shall briefly consider what others have said.

Lynn Scarlet observes that there is a food crisis in Africa which has nothing to do with "backwardness," "laziness," or inefficient farming techniques of the African farmers. In this she completely disagrees with other Africanists. Rather, among the chief causes of the crisis, she identifies (1) zealous planning

---

[14]*New York Times*, October 19, 1983. There were another twenty-two countries that were suffering from the severe effects of the crisis in 1973-1974.

[15]David N. Ballam and Michael J. Carey, *Food Politics: Regional Conflict* (Totowa, NJ: Osmun, 1981), 167.

[16]Radha Sinha, ed., *The World Food Problem: Consensus and Conflict* (New York: Pergamon Press, 1978), 448.

[17]Carlson has argued that (1) droughts are not the only source of famine; (2) famines can be dealt with, provided that proper plans are designed before they occur; (3) famine conditions mean that the total economic system is in serious trouble; (4) an interdependent collaboration is needed to understand the nature of famine and to prevent it; and (5) famines tend to threaten regimes. See Dennis G. Carlson, "Famine in History: With a Comparison of Two Modern Ethiopian Disasters," in *Famine*, ed. Kevin M. Cahill (New York: Orbis Books, 1982), 14. See also Food and Agricultural Organization of the United Nations, *Famine in Africa: Situation, Cause, Prevention, Control*, 1982.

without necessary information, (2) ill-conceived economic planning, and (3) a bias against the production of luxury items.[18] The crisis could be remedied, she contends, if production of food is increased, which is "both a prerequisite and an impetus to improved distribution."[19] Furthermore, there is a growing need for the technical solution of Africa's natural problems. Equally and rightly stressed by Scarlet is the often neglected factor of senseless wars in East Africa, which drain the national budgets so much that when drought and famines occur, immediate solutions are rarely available. However, increasing the food supply is quite a difficult matter given the multiple problems initiated by political hierarchies, restrictions on credit, land use policies, state taxation, and agricultural procurement.[20] For Scarlet, these primary generators of inequality substantially account for the food problems. These food problems will not go away until an effort is made to establish agricultural market systems that really work. Her central conclusions are remarkably similar to Christensen's. Christensen also proposed the adoption of a "socially efficient" food market, as opposed to a "technically efficient" one, as the market system that would alleviate the food problem by shifting priority from "efficiency" to the satisfaction of human needs.[21]

There are surely considerable merits in these arguments. For example, both writers are sensitive to the need for paying close attention to "ideologically" motivated market structures such as those which are concerned only about "efficiency" at the expense of human justice (Christensen's argument), and the need to design

---

[18]Scarlet, "Tropical Africa," 174.

[19]Scarlet, "Tropical Africa," 174. As Scarlet put it, "Countries such as Zaire, Uganda and Ethiopia have suffered frequent interruption of more sophisticated means of transport such as roads and railways, especially as a result of wars and internal strife."

[20]Scarlet, "Tropical Africa," 176-77.

[21]For Christensen, a "socially efficient" food system is one in which production and distribution of at least basic food staples to a total population is accomplished with the smallest possible use of resources. See Cheryl Christensen, "World Hunger: A Structural Approach," in Hopkins and Puchala, 748. For a similar argument, see Scarlet, 178-79.

market systems that truly work, although the meaning of "true" is undetermined (Scarlet's perspective). These arguments, though useful, ultimately are inadequate since they suggest incremental changes rather than structural changes.

In a very stimulating and thoughtful work Robert Bates has argued that food crisis can be caused by the political strategies of policy makers, when policy makers prevent farmers from determining what they should produce, the conditions under which they produce, and to whom cash crops are sold.[22] Where producers lack the freedom to produce food, they correspondingly lack the incentive to produce goods and move commodities. Bates rightly identifies the lack of incentives as one of the most powerful reasons why farmers do not produce in quantities that would effectively protect African economics from periodic crises.

Furthermore, the plan of modernizing African economies by focusing on "industry" has a devastating impact on agriculture. African policy makers are notorious for taking over the marketing boards in Africa which originated historically to function as trustees of farmers by taking accumulated funds to develop industry. Through this means, it was easy to produce the food crisis. When poor farmers acutely sense the implications of this strategy, they do not push themselves to produce as much food as they could. They refuse, to paraphrase Theodore Schultz, "to turn sand into gold." Worst of all, poor farmers, as Bates indicates with a plethora of examples from Nigeria and Ghana, hopelessly involve themselves in the corrupting process of bribing marketing officials to enable them to sell their food products illegally for higher prices to whomever pays, then benefitting themselves when their landless brothers and sisters are suffering acutely from hunger. The well-to-do farmers then contribute to the food crisis as opposed to getting victimized by it, as the poor (landless and moneyless) peasants do. Without exaggeration, as I have argued above, and as Bates powerfully proves, the most pitiable victims of the aggressive and corrupt interventions of government to control the production and pricing of food in the agricultural sector are the poor peasants, and not the most privileged lords of the countryside. Of course,

---

[22]Robert Bates, *Markets and States in Tropical Africa* (Berkeley: University of California Press, 1984).

13

it is obvious as well that the poor urban dwellers suffer from the corrupt and greedy mechanisms of the market systems in Africa. As Bates put it, "the policy responses of African governments to the problem of urban food supply thus appear to be leading to the entrance in the countryside of politically influential elites—elites who seek to make their fortunes by engaging in food production, and who adopt farming technologies that fundamentally alter the social and economic patterns of the African countryside."[23] These urban elites as well as their vigorous allies—as they claim, the privileged farmers—are draining African economies rather than with commitment and vision energizing Africa's abundant but abused material resources. The various political strategies by which African officials, the urban consumers of food at *low cost*, as well as the privileged farmers, contribute to the food crisis is intelligently documented by Bates.

What Africa needs is not the development of industries but rather an intelligent development of agriculture—one which could sufficiently feed, clothe, and shelter each and every human being in Africa. The possibility of transforming African agriculture to the *equal* benefit of all its citizens, however, requires nothing short of reorienting our deeply entrenched way of looking at food as nothing more than a commodity.

Sarah Berry, in a very powerful work marked by the acumen of shrewd observation, *Fathers Work For Their Sons*, has also studied the abuse of resources in the Nigerian political scene. Her thesis and conclusions may be summarized as follows. Nigerian businessmen as well as their privileged counterparts in Yorubaland have not always used the capital accumulated from the oil boom of the 1970s and the impressive production of cocoa for the full-scale development of Yorubaland. Rather, many farmers were forced to leave the land and migrate to the cities to find employment in the lucrative job of fixing the cars of the privileged lords of the city. Not all those who leave the land and move to the cities, however, are fortunate enough to find jobs. Jobs, in the Nigerian context as a whole, are related to kinship. Even fathers work for their sons, so that their sons, the fathers hope, can move up the social ladder by accumulating the appropriate university

---

[23]Bates, *Markets*, 60.

14

degrees and by establishing contacts with those who control jobs. It is as if those who are not related to the city sophisticates are barred from succeeding in the Nigerian social political scene. The case of the Yorubaland shows succinctly how hegemonic ideas are used to enable some to be solvent and mobile and to condemn others to remain at their miserable politically/economically determined stations which some people accept as their fate. Sarah Berry's book is a powerful documentation of the operation of corruption and the cunning of political reason in the hands of the extremely enterprising Nigerian politicians.

I contend, however, that incremental changes are hardly enough to overcome the food crisis; at issue is the need to fundamentally reorient our attitudes about how food is produced, exchanged, distributed, and consumed. Food is part of a process which is conditioned by ideologies and specific political decisions. In what follows, I will use Hegel's notion of immediacy (something that is out there and is taken for granted) to penetrate the complex process of understanding what food is and what food is not, or to be more precise, what food is immediately considered to be and what food truly is when we reflect about it.

When food is viewed in its immediacy, it is simply considered a thing, an object of consumption.[24] However, food is not simply a thing; rather, it is a concrete result of a very complex human activity. It is, simply put, a product of human labor power. To that extent, food is produced under some purposefully and thoughtfully designed modes of production.

Food then, when nonreflectively (immediately) looked at, is nothing more than an object of consumption, a "thing" to be bought and sold as any other commodity. Upon deep and conscious reflection, however, food becomes visible as the ultimate product of ideologically conditioned mediate processes under

---

[24]Immediacy is a central Hegelian notion. By immediacy, Hegel understands a process in which we unreflectively absorb all that we experience in the world as given, as "simple and indeterminate" as he put it in the beginning section of Being. The object of philosophy is to transform being, the stage of immediacy to the Idea, the realm of true knowledge. For a discussion of immediacy within the context of Being, the first moment of the Idea, see the section on Being pp. 125-61. William Wallace, trans., *Hegel's Logic* (Oxford: Clarendon Press, 1975).

which it is produced, distributed, exchanged, and consumed. In other words, we begin to see food mediately as a concrete result of a totality of processes and ideologies.[25] When we view the African food crisis mediately, we come to realize that the crisis hides a complex of factors that are not readily accessible to observation, but which can be grasped by thought. For example, what we cannot see is the objectivity of the production process, and the set of man-made laws that determine how food, a product of human labor, is to be used and exchanged. In this view, although food has both a use value and an exchange value, often it is its exchangeability that reigns supreme. Its "natural end" is often neglected. Food, like any other commodity, has to be exchanged for money.

Earlier we contended that a food crisis occurs when sale and purchase are separated. We now add that this way of looking at the food crisis is to consider food itself as nothing more than a commodity. But, what is a commodity? From Marx, we learn that "a commodity appears, at first sight, a very trivial thing, and easily understood."[26] But he concludes, upon a deep analysis we could discover that a

> commodity is therefore a mysterious thing, simply
> because in it the social character of men's labor

---

[25]See the introduction to the *Grundrisse* by Marx for a precise discussion of the notion of totality. Consider this passage for example: "The conclusion we reach is not that production, distribution, exchange and consumption are identical, but that they all form the members of a totality, distinctions within a unity. Production predominates not over itself, in the antithetical definition of production, but over the other moments as well." See Karl Marx, *Grundrisse*, trans. Martin Nicolans (New York: Vintage Books, 1973), 99. We presuppose this particular framework by Marx, which he inherited and transformed from Hegelian logic, when we contend that food is a concrete totality—a totality whose various parts are production, distribution, exchange, and consumption. When crisis occurs, there is an inevitable crisis of production, distribution, exchange, and consumption. Non-Marxian economists still continue to separate the parts of the totality.

[26]Karl Marx, *Capital*, ed. Frederick Engels, vol. 1 (New York: International Publishers, 1974), 71.

16

appears to them as an objective character stamped upon the product of that labor: because the relation of the producers to the sum total of their own labor is presented to them as a social relation, existing not between themselves, but between the products of their labor.[27]

If Marx's conception of the commodity makes sense, then we can now argue that food is more than a thing that is sold, a thing out there, outside of us the human laborers. It is an indispensable and inseparable aspect of human biological life. Food, by virtue of its nature, belongs to the realm of the inalienable basic rights of humankind. Surely, we can grasp this particular nature of food not when we view it in its immediacy, but only when we think of it as a culmination of a process, a producer of life in its plenitude.

During moments of economic crisis, we can think of the problem on two levels. The first level is to think out the objective reasons behind the crisis. This is what economists attempt to do from different economic perspectives, some of which we have reviewed earlier. The second level is to ask oneself in what way does it affect me, or what are my obligations such that the crisis could be properly analyzed and perhaps be alleviated? The first level is an attempt to penetrate the ideas that underlie the objective economic process. The second is to begin transforming the crisis from the realm of a remote event—in the case occurring somewhere in Africa—directly to one's self as a member of humankind.

We shall illustrate this first level with an abstract example from Africa. With the exception of those countries that call themselves socialist, and which also are suffering from the food crisis, the producers of food either work for those who live in the city but own land in the country, or are self-employed as part-time farmers and part-time workers. For us, full-time food producers are the relevant types of producers—that is, those who do not own the land but work for those who do. We are also concerned with those who own land and sell the produce to domestic and world markets. These are the markets that exploit the landless peasants

---

[27]Marx, *Capital*, 72.

by making profit or by providing techniques and technologies that are beyond the means of the primary producers and which they can afford only at a sacrifice.

Landless peasants produce for two markets. The first is the national or domestic market; African landowning peasants hire landless peasants. In return for the labor which the hired peasants provide, they receive money as well as some of the produce. The wage and produce payment, following Marx's theory of labor value, is not equivalent or is not a just measure of the amount of labor that the landless peasants are expending. The systematic process of exploitation to which they are being subjected, however, is justified as natural, as a contractual relationship between the landless peasants and their wealthy employers. The employers make it evident to their employees that their generosity of providing work could be discontinued any time and that the peasants' labor is dispensable, so dispensable that there are many other peasants that are ready to accept what some peasants reject. The world of the landless peasants is a world of intimidation, uncertainty, and anxiety; their employers know this.

Landless peasants are also exploited internationally at the hands of capital. The exploitative wages and grain that the landless peasants receive in the countryside frequently are insufficient for them to live on. Consequently, they are compelled to go to the city to become seasonal employees in factories, or to work as guards, janitors, houseboys, masons, escorts, or gardeners. In this way, the country peasants gradually become city workers. As workers, particularly as factory workers, the exploitation of peasants becomes identical to the classical experience of workers in the history of Europe. The peasants thus are doubly exploited: as landless peasants in the hands of rural landlords, and as workers in the hands of capital in the city. By the peasants' participation efforts, the rural landlords are enriched; the peasants' work in the city results in the accumulation of capital and therefore the extraction of surplus labor from the peasants as seasonal workers.

To simplify the discussion and to draw the hegemonic vision to the discussion, both the African peasant and those for whom he or she produces and to whom he or she often sells are participating in an objective economic process in which the production of surplus values, profits, capital, and interest is the central and deeply held principle that guides their everyday life.[28] These people are participating in a process in which they are not reflective or fully conscious subjects. For them, to acquire the necessary human qualities of reflection, morality, and consciousness, they need to understand the inner architectonic of economic theories that underlies the capitalist mode of production as the end, as the nature-given way under which human labor is to be organized. Poor peasants are too busy making a living to concern themselves with informing their minds with the conceptualizing of their misery. They complain not because they theoretically understand but rather because they suffer directly. Experience is their teacher.

The peasant producers, as much as those who purchase their products in market economies, have fully internalized the principles that govern the production of food as a commodity which may be called, for lack of better terms, capitalist ideas or alienated ideas. These ideas have become the leading values in Africa, where policymakers are essentially guided by these dominant, hegemonic theories. The poor peasants who labor on the land, and no longer produce surpluses, struggle to subsist under the natural mode of production. They too are guided by those unquestioned hegemonic principles. Here, we see a connection between the principles of the policymakers and the passive acceptance of these hegemonic theories by those formally uneducated and highly tradition-oriented peasants; one enforces the other. Of course, Bates is right however that poor farmers in tropical Africa do attempt to organize against the urban elites to help themselves, but the coalition of privileged consumers,

---

[28]There is of course a body of literature that treats the "peasant economy" as autonomous from capitalist economy. The peasant is not motivated by profit when he produces; instead, he produces enough to maintain his family; therefore, the capitalist principles do not apply to peasant economy. For a concrete summary of Chayanov's thesis described above, see David Lehmann, "After Chayanov and Lenin: New Paths of Agrarian Capitalism," *Journal of Development Economics* 2 (1982): 133-61. For a complete disagreement with Chayanov's thesis, see Lenin's arguments in V.T. Lenin, "The Development of Capitalism in Russia," in *Collected Works*, vol. 3 (London: Lawrence and Wishart, 1960), chapter 2, part 13.

privileged farmers, and government bureaucracies crushes them systematically.[29]

There are many cases in which this reciprocity of ideals works, in fact, to the disadvantage of the peasantry. This is the case when the peasantry actually is assimilating a world view that results in acceptance of material and nonmaterial exploitation or what we may call voluntary servitude. This voluntary servitude, however, is a result of ignorance combined with subjection to ideologies that systematically have infiltrated a civil society where tradition, custom, and religion grip the peasantry. The policy-makers, like the peasantry, have also assimilated these alienated ideas that benefit them monetarily (as opposed to intellectually or spiritually) but which also contribute toward the generation of the food crisis. During periods of crisis, we should not be surprised if we encounter some insensitive bureaucrats who take advantage of tragic human events.[30] The general conclusions we could draw from this discussion are as follows:

1.   The hegemonic ideas are clearly founded upon a systematic exploitation of some for the material satisfaction of others
2.   The beneficiaries of the ideas as much as the victims are ultimately not aware of the consequences to the same degree; the beneficiaries are blinded to the destructive consequence (to themselves) of starvation and death because

---

[29]Although the focus of this chapter is not limited to a particular country, the arguments about the situation in market economies may also apply to the situation in the socialist countries of Ethiopia, Tanzania, and Mozambique. See Robert Bates, *Markets and States in Africa* (Berkeley: University of California Press, 1981), 87-90; 106-19.

[30]In a very perceptive book, Markovitz has gone so far as to report the following alarming case in Chad: "Chad's newly overthrown profiters used their political position to gouge enormous profits out of the selling of relief food meant to relieve the misery of the starving." See Irving L. Markovitz, *Power and Class in Africa* (New Jersey: Prentice Hall, Inc., 1977), 348. For an excellent treatment of the impact of colonialism and imperialism, and the relationship of this argument to our hegemonic vision, see the discussion in chapter 3 in Markovitz, *Power and Class in Africa.*

they are deceived by material gains. The victims are passive ultimately because they are really misled perhaps by false rationalizations of the meaning of life

3.   Both the beneficiaries and victims are subjected to hegemonic ideas that generate alienation, passivity, and ignorance about one's place in the historical political space and in the relations of production

4.   The victims experience their problems as particular, private, and unsolvable since they consider those problems as results of nature.   The beneficiaries experience their gains as deserved and earned, given their education, skills, and merits which account for their positions of power

The challenge for the political philosopher is both to persuade the victims to view their experience as historically rather than naturally generated, and therefore discussable in the public political arena, and also to persuade the policymakers to transform these so-called natural, private problems to the public sphere of action. After this transformation, the policymakers themselves can be, if they so wish, retrained to decipher truth from falsehood, humanity from inhumanity, strategic politics from ethical politics, and compassion from greed. We will pursue this theme on a higher level of abstraction in the following section. Before we move on, we shall briefly summarize the discussions of the first two parts of this chapter.

First, the basic idea behind the concept of hegemony is that men and women are not governed by material/economic forces alone, but also by ideas. The significance of material concerns becomes important in the last instance only after the ideas that those material concerns harbor are revealed to their conscious minds. To this insight, we gave the name of the counterhegemonic vision. Second, we argued that a comprehensive assessment of the African food crisis requires the illuminating power of the counterhegemonic vision, which may help us to assess critically the form, content, and the implicit and explicit goals in some of the most dominant economic theories, of which the prevailing economic theories in Africa are reflections. The third point is that given the dominant market-oriented economic theories on the global level—free enterprise and central command theories and their popularity in the African scene—any food crisis there rather quickly demands the disclosure of those unexamined economic presuppositions of treating food as a commodity and the subsequent resultant of alienation. The fourth contention is that in addition to the human-caused generation of the food crisis, there also are other determinants of the food crisis—soil erosion, population growth, partial and insensitive bureaucracy, one-sided and ill-conceived economic plans, primitive technology, and science. However, we contend that these other determinants may be controllable by some intelligent technical and technological innovations.

The Notion of Counterhegemonic Vision

> Justice depends on my respecting the rights of others. It is a virtue if I regard it as a duty and make it the maxim of my actions not because the state so requires but simply because it is a duty, and in that event it is a requirement of the moral law, not of the state.
>
> Hegel

The two important questions in this section are (1) should food be a subject of ideology, or is it beyond ideology but constitutive of humanity? and (2) how can Africans help themselves and what can the members of the human community, particularly the intellectuals, do to contribute toward the prevention of the food crisis?

Our response to question (1) may be stated as follows: If our analysis of the food crisis makes sense, to the extent that food is considered a commodity, it easily follows that food becomes a subject for ideology—governed by the economic principles of profit maximization and capital accumulation. Food also becomes an instrument of foreign policy. Empirically speaking, food still continues to be a subject of ideology; and the food crisis in Africa is analyzed less from humanitarian and moral perspectives than from economic, scientific, technological, and political ones. From the perspective of the counterhegemonic vision, we call these types of analyses ideological.

Following the thesis of the counterhegemonic vision, we will contend that in spite of the empirical categorization of the African

22

food crisis, it is possible to reconceptualize it from a humanitarian/ moral perspective. This perspective by no means neglects economic, technological, and scientific dimensions; it simply reveals the deep ethical, philosophic, and religious structures of the crisis. It subsequently considers the economic aspect of the food crisis as significantly unavoidable only in the last instance. From a cause-and-effect perspective, we contend that the food crisis is an effect of regarding food as a commodity and alienation of food as such, the divorce of the food crisis from the silent and unobservable moral and human laws that alienated human beings do not fully comprehend. We begin with a discussion of the mentality and world views of the African peasantry and decision makers, which is the issue of question (2) above.

In the final analysis, only Africans themselves can overcome the food crisis by their productive activities and their relationships with each other within their local, regional, national, and international markets, and their relationship with food producers on a global level. This self-understanding requires the mastery of a complex network of relationships in an interdependent world. Additionally, and this is very important, the peasantry and African decision makers need to master the meaning of the ideas that underlie the workings of political economy, both the economic categories of political economy and the ethical, philosophical, psychological, and political dimensions of the economic categories themselves. Such a self-understanding would require a long-range project guided by the possibility of consciousness raising. Such a potential activity may be captured by another simplifying term, which we would call a counterhegemonic vision, the goal of which we shall discuss below. By counterhegemonic vision, we simply mean a project, a task for the future. It is an attempt to construct an alternative view of development that is capable of overcoming poverty and hunger.

In the world of food production, a majority of the peasantry must produce to sustain themselves as well as produce surpluses for the national market and the world market. In the act of production for two markets, there are at least two modes of exploitation to which the peasantry is subjected. The first type was described earlier as commodification of food, in which food is primarily viewed as a thing, thereby hiding the deep human social relations that food establishes by production and reproduction of life as such. This deep level, however, could be revealed only if we unmask the "thinghood" of food. This may be done by the process of consciousness transformation; that is, counter-hegemonic vision. The second level of exploitation, on the other hand, could be grasped at the outset by a critical discussion of the process of production that is peculiar to capitalism, which is gradually but surely penetrating the world of the autonomous peasant producers. The peasant is not just producing exclusively for his subsistence and his family any longer; he is producing for a network of other human agents—the local landlords, the city capitalists, for whom he occasionally works to sustain the plots of land that the peasant owns or rents, or for the state (in socialist economies). As he engages in these activities, the process of alienation is at work which Marx so movingly describes in the *Economic and Philosophical Manuscripts* of 1844.[31] There Marx describes at least five forms of alienation: alienation from self, from productive activity, from fellow workers, from the human species, and from nature. The African peasant, we contend, is alienated in these five senses, given the basic premise that his produce (particularly cash crops) is no longer his, but is produced for a market. From this process of alienation, we derive the other forms of alienation to which the peasant is unconsciously subjected. Our central contention here of course is that the African peasant is not aware of how the two processes of exploitation—the commodification of food and the extraction of surplus for the purposes of capital accumulation—really work.[32] Both processes are hidden

---

[31]These arguments were fully expanded by Marx first in the *Economic and Philosophical Manuscripts* of 1844, then in the *Grundrisse* of 1857, and finally in the section on Commodities in the *Capital*, vol. 1. Many of Marx's insights about alienated labor occur in this chapter to illuminate the African food crisis. For a discussion of Marx on humanitarian philosophy, see Erich Fromm, *Marx's Concept of Man* (New York: Unger, 1973). For a detailed discussion of alienation, see Tedros Kiros, "Toward a Construction of a Theory of Alienation in Aesthetics: Marx, Tolstoy and Benjamin" (M.A. thesis, Kent State University, 1982).

[32]See the highly perceptive discussions and documentation of how the peasantry is exploited by the rural landlords and by the state

by the function of alienation as ideology. This process is so much hidden from the critical understanding of the peasantry that the peasantry does not really possess an understanding of the economic reasons that generate the African food crisis.

Rather, when life's agonies become unbearable, when famines strike, and when the food crisis affects everyday life, poetry instead of science, distorted religion instead of rational thinking, resignation instead of critical activity, and despair instead of hope become the peasant's only guides. On this point, according to one unique account in early 1974, an expatriate said during a national conference on the famine that he believed God was trying to teach the nation by means of famine.[33] Here, we see the power of ideology and the unnecessary complications that it brings to the lives of those who are suffering from secular problems. What is particularly vivid here is the human disposition to assign the unknown causes of a phenomenon to God as if God is irrational, cruel, and the embodiment of unintelligence. Such distorted interpretations of God, and therefore of religion, were disputed by one of Ethiopia's spiritual leaders, a wise philosopher. He wrote, "He [God] is intelligent who understands all, for He created us intelligent from the abundance of his intelligence. . . God did not create me intelligent without a purpose, that is to look for Him and to grasp Him and there is wisdom in the path that He has opened for me." Zara Yaoqob, the philosopher, then asked, "Why is it that all men do not adhere to truth, instead of [believing] falsehood?" He speculates that the reason seemed to be "the nature of man which is weak and sluggish. Man aspires to know truth and the hidden things of nature, but his endeavor is difficult

---

machinery that buys the local products at extremely cheap price in collaboration with the wealthy classes of the foreign importers of cheap food in Lehmann, "After Chayanov," 147-49, 154-57. Lehmann does not specifically write about the African peasantry, but it is reasonable to assume that with minor variations what is true of the peasantry elsewhere is also true of the peasantry in Africa. For parallel discussions of this phenomenon in the African case, see Markovitz, *Power and Class*, 83-97.

[33]Carlson, "Famine in History," in *Famine*, ed. Kevin M. Cahill, 14.

and can only be grasped with great labor and patience."[34] In that mode, religion feeds upon ideology's mystifying function. In the form of an irrational belief, religion can easily be employed to account for famines and food crises as events that cannot be averted.[35] Following the potential use of counterhegemonic vision, we can assert by making the philosopher's meditations our own that when religion becomes not merely blind belief but rational faith, it demystifies reality; it genuinely struggles to explain the structure and intelligibility of this "immediately" irrational but potentially knowable world. The meaning of the partly natural and partly human phenomenon called food crisis, within the context of such a rational framework, gives rise to insights by which future disasters may be avoided. These insights may of course require both "redemption" and critical consciousness transformation in the form of rational and conscious political action.

The transformation of consciousness from the stage of mere belief to the stage of rational knowledge is an excruciating experience; it demands that seemingly impossible but sincere quest to penetrate the nature of the intelligence itself so as to overcome the spell of falsehood. It is falsehood that persistently impels the African peasantry to render the food crisis a natural aspect of being. Thought, when genuinely exercised—that is, when it is freed from the self-imposed domination of ideology—enables us to innovate and to imagine, and has the power to stimulate us toward autonomy.

When thought grips the peasantry, they will begin to see the network of interconnections between their immediate surroundings, the village, and the complex world of which the village is a part. Specifically, they will begin to see the way in which positive

---

[34]Zara Yaoqob, "The Treatise of Zara Yaoqob," *Ethiopian Philosophy* (Addis Ababa: Commercial, 1978), 8.

[35]Carlson, noting the effects of religious ideas upon secular events, has reported that "during both famines, a traditional world view was expressed in which drought and famine were believed by a large part of the population to be part of the judgment and punishment of God for human sin, with a sense that little could be done to avert or minimize such divine action." See Carlson, "Famine in History," in *Famine*, ed. Kevin M. Cahill, 14.

religion[36] has been interpreted for it by the powers that be, the village priests, and the religious chiefs, and how this interpretation ultimately contributes toward the justification of terrestrial suffering—poverty, disease, and famines. Similarly, the peasantry might begin to see the subtle connections between the distorted religious forms and some of the hegemonic economic theories that solidify and legitimize themselves by directly referring to the great books of religion. When the peasantry becomes enlightened the meaning of the food crisis takes a radically different meaning to them. Likewise, the peasantry's world would radically change. The peasants expand their horizon; they deindividualize their understanding; they might begin to see the interpenetration of private and public everyday experiences; they reevaluate their provinciality; they might begin consciously to increase their productivity, thereby contributing not just toward capital accumulation for others but toward adequately feeding themselves and all those who are hungry for food. In particular (and this is our central argument here) critical thought as an aspect of the counterhegemonic vision which is critical to enlightenment is possible only (1) when the effects of distorted religion are overcome through gradual stages, (2) when critical thought is expressed in responsible and well-organized forms of political action that demand a viable political space, and (3) where the hunger for justice and the access to all the technological forces that would render adequate food production are guaranteed. We will now elaborate the first point. As to the second and third points, elaborations will be made in the concluding remarks.

It is perhaps possible to convince all traditional hegemonic thinkers in Africa in general, the members of civil society and political society, and the peasantry in particular that the food crisis is not exclusively a natural problem. It is a problem that is subject to change by critically thinking and willing human beings. It may be possible to persuade the peasantry (by designing educational apparatus within civil society) to digest some of the meditative thoughts of Zara Yaoqob in which it is implicitly suggested that the

---

[36]For an excellent interpretation of positive religion, in remarks that strikingly parallel Zara Yaoqob's, see the early works of Frederick Hegel, *On Christianity: Early Theological Writings*; trans. T.M. Knox (New York: Harper & Brothers, 1961).

27

creator who endowed us with superior human intelligence would not tolerate the abuse of that intelligence—that is, the repudiation of the autonomous power to think for ourselves. The intelligence given to us must categorically command us to produce food as abundantly as is necessary presuming that our capacity to imagine, to create, and to work for humanity is at full force.[37] If we come to religion through individual critical thought instead of through the interpretation of others, if the use of our intelligence results in producing food for everybody instead of for the hegemonic capitalistic market, then we will have created one of the most necessary prerequisites of the possibility of a civilized life—a life in which we do not have to worry about food, the most elementary and indispensable human need. It is precisely because of the elementary and necessary nature of food that we think of it not just as a subject for political economy, but as constitutive of humanity.

The central duty that Africans have to themselves then is to become critically knowledgeable about what they can do and what they might be unable to do so that the food crisis in Africa can be alleviated. This duty requires, among other things, a dispassionate look at the life conditions of the peasantry—a life of material and religious exploitation; a selfless examination of economic theories; and an examination of the ideas of the African bureaucrats who lead Africa both domestically and internationally. It is precisely inside these centers of power that we might ultimately find the key to solve the African food crisis by the sincere efforts of Africans themselves—peasantry, city representatives, leaders, spokespersons, and scholars.

Researching these local centers of power is to gradually learn about the effects of the hegemonic ideas, and to engage in the counterhegemonic vision. Africans could thereby design new institutions, innovate appropriate new theories that would serve Africa and also the world which depends on Africa's resources. However, before Africa could do any of the above tasks, it has to construct a self-sufficient ethical African community. This is, of course, not an easy task; nonetheless the groundwork for the

---

[37]For a detailed discussion of the categorical imperative and its function in human life, particularly in ethical/moral theories, see Immanuel Kant, *Foundations of the Metaphysics of Morals* (Indianapolis: The Bobbs-Merrill Company, 1975), 22-85.

future possibility of an ethical community must begin now. It may begin with Africans who enlighten themselves by their own efforts. The fundamental need in Africa now more than ever before is enlightenment grounded upon the counterhegemonic vision.

Enlightenment, Kant tells us, is "humanity's emergence from self-incurred tutelage." In Africa's case, there is a special form of dependency in self-incurred tutelage to ideas that have long hidden the real causes and the determinants of hunger. One of the aims of this book has been an attempt to shed light on this problem by analyzing certain key questions. Self-education is one of the most effective forms of enlightenment. Its necessary condition is that one at least desires to be educated. The presence of this condition cannot be assumed in the African context; to bring it about is a task, a project. In Africa, there has long prevailed a particular form of education, that is, education to dependency. But education to dependency is not education at all in the critical sense; it is really what some people call indoctrination or, put mildly, socialization. True education, whatever else it may be, is absolutely resistant to dependency, where dependency is the expression of nonfreedom. But freedom is the necessary condition for the possibility of education, and it is only when we guarantee freedom's existence that we can conduct the demanding task of enlightenment. In Africa, both the condition of freedom (freedom from dependency) and the task of enlightenment have yet to take place. Due to the powerful presence of hegemonic ideologies that indoctrinate to dependency, there is an indispensable need to start from the beginning. Indoctrination to ideologies ought to be replaced by education to freedom, the freedom to think for oneself, to persistently and courageously struggle to disclose the hidden meaning of ideas—religious, political, economic, and philosophical.

To think freely is to ask, to interrogate, to investigate, to test one's convictions, beliefs, and modes of behavior. It is ultimately to seek to know who one is, who one was, and who one might possibly become. It would be, we might add, a sincere attempt to reconstruct one's history on the basis of studying the past, questioning the present, and envisioning the future.

The African material and ideological present is a web of its past and the unknown future. If we are right in imputing to hegemonic ideology a powerful role in the formation of Africa's past history, a history in which religious forces in particular have played a crucial part, and if we are right in our assertion that the history of the past has now spilled over into the present, then it follows that the hegemonic ideology has spilled over into its present. The past and the present, however, would still have an effect on the unknown future. If the past and the present contribute toward the perpetuation of dependency on ideas, the nature of which is not critically understood, then the future would still be impacted by the past and present ideologies that are simply a priori hostile to enlightenment and the consequent role of imagination. It is because of the need of imaging the possibilities of the future in a novel and autonomous way that we are suggesting here, following Kant, that African producers and leaders alike take on the demanding task of enlightening the populace through the reinfiltration of counterhegemonic ideas to the spheres of Africa's civil and political societies. This is the concrete goal of the counterhegemonic vision; in this project, enlightenment ought to play a foundational role.

Among other things, to engage in such a counterhegemonic vision is to investigate the objective circumstance of natural resources, the necessary condition for the prevention of the food crisis, and thus the possibility of a civilized life in the poverty-stricken continent. If the much-needed natural resources are there but the necessary condition—the presence of critical thinking—is not readily available, then it would follow that those who are affected by hunger need to engage in responsible and rational political action. In this situation, self-education plays the significant role of inciting the affected human subjects to go to the political sphere. There, through speaking and acting, they make their demands heard, or to use the the language of counterhegemony, they explode the world of irrational and alienating ideas.[38] They make it clear to themselves that they have long believed in falsehoods, the primary popularizers of which were they themselves as passive believers and promoters. If the habits of exploding irrational ideas take root in the life of the African subjects, rational political action—the privileged virtue of men and women—gradually replaces

---

[38]I am indebted to the writings of Hannah Arendt, who pioneered the view that political action is superior to any other kind of action; it humanizes the needs of modern man. See Hannah Arendt, *The Human Condition* (Chicago: The University of Chicago Press, 1958).

the deadly poison of political passivity. Wrong-headed political action originating in African leadership systems exacerbates the food crisis just as much as inaction and political passivity paralyze it. We need to come up with alternative forms of political action grounded upon critical ideas and guided by participatory political institutions, neither one of which is presently available to the peasantry.

But in Africa, even rational political action embodied in participatory political institutions is hardly enough to alleviate the food crisis. Rational political action may satisfy the subjective needs of the hungry—surely it will make them feel good—but it will hardly show them those various technical ways by which they could satisfy their need for food. The latter can be best accomplished in formal educational institutions. There is a desperate need for moral, political, technical, and scientific education. Numerous scholars in the field have called for a massive reeducation of Africans, particularly of food producers. In particular, the students of the African food crisis have made the central point that African food systems are backward; they need the blessing of modern technology.[39] We agree with this central point. However, we caution that not all kinds of technology are suitable for Africa; some will do more damage than good. If the future technocrats of Africa were nurtured with a proper training in moral philosophy, they would be well-equipped to choose morally sensitive technology. The most appropriate forms of technology for Africa need to be in the areas of transportation, communication, and food storage capacity.[40]

The tenor of the above suggestions is the accurate view that nature in Africa is technologically incompletely transformed. Surely, this less-than-complete transformation is hardly a virtue. A potential transformation of nature with the requisite ethical restraint ought to be among the foremost components of a counterhegemonic project. The need to transform nature without

---

[39]For a very good discussion of this theme, see Rene Dumont and Bernard Rosier, *The Hungry Future* (New York: Praeger Publishers, 1968).

[40]See Food and Agricultural Organization of the U.N., *Famine in Africa*.

making it hostile to the African laborers is again a necessary condition for the possibility of a materially civilized life. If it were possible to transform nature without losing its closeness to humankind, since humans also are the conscious expression of nature, we could hypothesize here that a materially and spiritually civilized life in Africa, particularly in its precapitalistic sectors, may harbor a truly new life for humankind. Above, we have suggested how Africans themselves might be able to handle the food crisis and outlined some tentative hypothetical proposals.

Earlier, we cautiously implicated the role of international trade in the generation of Africa's food crisis. Recall that African domestic products find their way to the international markets which, among other things, extract surplus value from peasant economies. To that extent, the international markets contribute to the generation of the food crisis through the intricate roles of domestic bureaucrats and foreign corporations.[41] We are now contending that through a gradual moral and political education, the wealthy sectors of the industrial technological West can contribute toward the alleviation of the African food crisis. Here, consciousness raising plays a vital role.

For example, Rawls' book, *A Theory of Justice*, provides a model of how the members of humankind, those who have a capacity for a sense of justice, may bring about a just society—the chief features of which are the extension of the basic liberties and economic and social opportunities for all. If we are to extend the thesis of his book to the world community of which Africa is a part, we may be able to approach the food crisis as a question of social justice. Food, we might contend, is an uncompromising need of all those who have been badly treated by life. Social justice, we might further assert, has to see to it that all those who cannot produce enough to eat and thus suffer from the food crisis are helped in such a way as to alleviate the crisis once and for all. Those wealthy members of humankind, given their positive circumstance, ought to help others. The others may in turn respond by actively developing the necessary conditions for them to be genuinely self-determining. The capacity for a sense of justice will

---

[41]See footnote 31. Lehmann, "After Chayanov," argues the point on pp. 133-34.

draw the former to come to the help of the latter since the condition in which the latter find themselves is not their own doing, but is conditioned by the permeation of ideas that continue to destroy them. Of course, the positively circumstanced are not the conscious originators of the ideas. Thus, what is needed is not accusation, but cooperation, cooperation that is grounded upon the moral power of men and women directed toward the construction of a relatively abundant human community in which men and women do not have to worry about their most elementary needs.[42] Rawls' book is a truly ambitious work in ethical theory. A book of this type has the power to revitalize men and women to reflect as moral beings, with the consequent freedom to think about the plight of all those who are suffering, those who are still hungry for food and thirsty for the water of social justice. We shall revive this theme in our last chapter.

The other form of education that needs to be made accessible to humankind is genuine political education, and this is the function of that concept about which we have said enough— hegemony and its opposite, counterhegemony. Through the media of counterhegemonic institutions of political and civil societies in the West as well as the East, counterproductive ideas that emphasize our our dissimilarities need to be questioned. The negative and destructive effects that they tend to produce in Africa need to be revealed, publicized, and freely discussed in the great

---

[42]For a remarkable philosophical account of the way in which fraternity might rationally function as the basis for the abolition of hunger in an ethically sensitive community, see the remarks scattered throughout the article by Andreas Eshete, "Fraternity," *The Review of Metaphysics* 35/1 (1981): 27-45. See particularly pp. 32-33. Whereas Eshete uses hunger as an example of how members of a social union come to see the bond that ties them and makes them brothers, fraternity is ultimately the most powerful moral force which we have and which ties us to the material and nonmaterial circumstances of humankind. The food crisis of Africa is also the potential crisis of humankind; amoral political economy alienates us from one another further and further by magnifying our divisions and mystifying our fraternity. See also Johnson Nicholson and Ralph L. Nicholson, *Agriculture, Food and Human Values* (Indiana: Prudue University Press, 1979), 6-8, 118-24, 174-80, 216, 218-20.

academic centers of the West and the East. The function of education may perhaps become the objective examination of hegemonic ideas. Their findings may eventually reach the citizens, and the citizens will then become truly informed about the facts of the human condition. They will thus become politically informed. True political information is a necessary, though not sufficient, condition for the possibility of political education. Political education is the painful work of political philosophers in concert with the citizens who demand guidance from others in their quest for self-enlightenment. True political education is self-imposed and self-guided. In that case the political philosopher's duty can be providing not *what* individuals must think, but *how* they must think when they want to think. The political philosopher can prepare individuals to lead the demanding task of living as responsible and autonomous citizens. Again, the above remarks are intended to be brief outlines of how political education may be obtained. Humankind may thus be drawn to reflect and act upon the problems of the African food crisis through the concentric roles of moral and political education.

Food and Morality

The African food crisis clearly affects an overwhelming number of Africans who are suffering from hunger. In spite of the food crisis, however, the commodification of food in the African precapitalist sectors seems to be misplaced. When people are hungry, when they do not know how to live from day to day, it hardly makes sense to decorate African cities with ostentatious displays of wealth: boxing arenas, cars, and swimming pools. Decorations perhaps should be replaced by food items, internal wars should give way to the reappropriation of the national budgets toward the technical, scientific, and ethical reeducation of the food producers and the political administrators who allocate the goods. Finally, inadequate and ideologically motivated theories need to be scrutinized, critically interpreted, and thoughtfully studied before they penetrate the African political and civil societies.

The feeding and clothing of the genuinely needy victims of the African food crisis should not be the subject of ideology; having food is a basic human right. In saying this, we attempt to

34

dissuade the powerful nations of the world from looking at food as an instrument of foreign policy, a tool with which those nations which comply with the ideologies of the powerful are rewarded and those who dissent are punished.[43] For those who are hungry, food is more than a need. It is necessary for them to live the free life that is worthy of them as spiritual beings. For the poor African farmers, true freedom is yet in the future; given their poverty-stricken existence, they cannot even imagine a life of freedom. Yet, this state of darkness under which they spend their lives is unnatural and beyond their control. It is man-made; therefore it could be changed by man. That intelligence which generates the food crisis is the same intelligence, ethically informed and motivated, that could alter it.

Food should be beyond ideology, although a food crisis is a product of ideology. The basic right to which all human beings are entitled, the right to eat by virtue of the fact that they are, as Kant said, a "Kingdom of ends," must encompass the African victims of the food crisis. They deserve to live a decent life and one day, when the material conditions of civilization mature, they may live the "good" life as well. Continuous research about technical scientific possibilities by which Africans ought to feed themselves are categorical imperatives that need no scientific justification. The need to feed the hungry is a categorically binding human task, a task to which the East and the West as members of the human community need to be sensitive.[44]

However much one might disagree with the concept of hegemony, which serves as our point of view in this book, we might gain one fundamental wisdom from it, namely, that when an unexamined idea, which may give rise to the internalization of beliefs, becomes fully disclosed, it may become a source of shame, a source of self-disrespect. When we gradually become aware and embrace consciousness, we may realize how wrong we have been, how immoral the consequences of our actions were and how much we did not know. But not to know is just as harmful as to know

---

[43]For an enlightening discussion, see William Schneider, *Food, Foreign Policy and Raw Materials and Cartels* (New York: Crane, Rossack, 1976).

[44]See Dumont and Rosier, *The Hungry Future*.

and yet to do things that knowledge cannot bear. To be insensitive to the suffering of others belongs to the realm of not knowing and knowing at the same time. This happens only when we do not know the forceless force of ideas which regulate and dictate our actions; and it is precisely this insight that we gain from the concept of hegemony.

To think about starving men and women in Africa and then to engage in actively helping them is also to think about ourselves and to engage our "moral power" in a human task worthy of us.[45] It is in a way an attempt to humanize ourselves by removing the dehumanizing conditions under which others live. The humanization of others is a necessary condition for the humanization of those of us who are not directly victimized by hunger, but only indirectly victimized by the dehumanization of others. The suffering of others also is our suffering just as the happiness of others may ultimately be a source of our own pride and happiness. Such is the future task, a task which we concretely outline through a programmatic discussion of principles in chapters 3 and 4. The food crisis in Africa is a crisis caused by the indifference of human beings both inside and outside of Africa. It is a moral crisis directly caused by the market that has disassociated morality from efficiency.

I will now move on to a detailed discussion of some of the main reasons which the literature has advanced in an attempt to explain the phenomenon of Africa's underdevelopment, limited here to the geneology of the "food crisis."

The thesis that I will attempt to advance in chapter 2 may be summarized as follows. The food crisis which we just analyzed from the angle of hegemonic ideology, which in the final analysis is influenced by economic infrastructure, impels us to delve deeper to the study of the elusive concept and practice of material underdevelopment. The food crisis, I will argue, is in fact deeply affected historically and morally by the African concept of the self, the African concept of external nature, and the consequent forms of the technological transformations of external nature that Africans adopted and failed to adopt prior to the appearance of

---

[45]I am indebted to John Rawls' *A Theory of Justice* (Cambridge: The Belknap Press of Harvard University Press, 1971), particularly chapter 9.

slavery and the penetration of colonialism and imperialism. The legacies of the African concept of self and external nature (internal factors) as well as the legacies of domestic and international slavery and colonialism continue to affect the human condition in Africa; the internal and external causes have in a spectacular way converged on the food crisis, a crisis for many Africans and for the non-Africans who continue to use Africa as a source of cheap labor and enormous natural resources.

A truly responsible way to understand the multiple causes of the prolonged and seemingly interminable presence of the food crisis is to look critically at the various ideas that have been tested against the African peasant economics with the intention of overcoming the deplorable facts of hunger and massive starvation. One excellent place to begin is once again to read and analyze the classic theories of development as they apply to the African experience with a focus on the food crisis.

2

TOWARD A THEORY OF
AFRICAN UNDERDEVELOPMENT

The relevant literature on Africa's underdevelopment is dominated by five theory-oriented schools of thought: (1) the modernization school, (2) the dependency school, (3) the political economy school, (4) the hegemony, ideology, and underdevelopment school, and (5) the classical political economy school.[1] Each of these schools claims to possess the most comprehensive theory explaining Africa's underdevelopment. Contrary to what each school says about the other schools which it criticizes, each of them in fact does make a substantial contribution toward the illumination of the whole. If Truth is a whole as some philosophers have contended, then that whole can be explained only by the conscious effort of not merely one school but of many schools, not merely one perspective but many perspectives. From this stand-point, the exclusive claims that the different schools have made would hardly satisfy the enormous task of developing a theory that adequately identifies the causes of Africa's underdevelopment. What is required then is the construction of a theory that combines into one "synthetic whole" the analytical contributions of the different schools of thought. The principle of hegemonic ideology may serve as that synthesizing whole which permeates the premises of the various schools of thought. This is our central contention at this juncture.

It is our thesis that the inclusion of a hegemonic ideology perspective would significantly contribute toward synthesizing the implicit ideas that are hidden in the theoretical orientations of the

---

[1]These are theoretical categories derived from the extensive literature which deals with Africa's underdevelopment.

different schools of thought. A clear discussion of the ideas of each school and how they are related to hegemonic ideology is the preliminary task in this chapter. The second major task is to synthesize a theory combining the insights of the different schools of thought under the umbrella of hegemonic ideology toward an explanation of Africa's underdevelopment. In this synthesis, the attempts of the various schools will be appraised and their conclusions will be incorporated into the hegemony/ideology perspective via constructive refutation. By constructive refutation, I mean the attempt at preserving the conceptual strengths of a given theory while constructively rejecting the inadequate premises and conclusions of that theory. In German, the word that describes this particular method of thinking is *Aufheben*. We employ this method in our attempts to construct a theory of Africa's underdevelopment via the incorporation of the premises of the schools of thought that we have identified under the guiding principles of hegemonic ideology and counterhegemonic vision.[2] It should be pointed out here, however, that we will focus only on the cause of Africa's underdevelopment; the important and much-needed theorizing about how Africa can be developed will not be touched upon. That topic will be examined in chapters 3 and 4.

Modernization and Hegemonic Ideology

The proponents of political-social-cultural development—Apter, Riggs, Black, and Einestadt—share the following theme: all the political systems of the world, those of the underdeveloped nations in particular, will have to go through the process that the developed nations have already undergone. The historical experiences of modernization—the discovery of science, labor

---

[2]For a detailed analysis of the concept of hegemony, see Tedros Kiros, *Toward the Construction of a Theory of Political Action; Antonio Gramsci: Consciousness, Participation and Hegemony* (Washington: University Press of America, 1985), particularly chapter 6. For special usage of the concepts of hegemonic ideology and counterhegemonic vision, see Tedros Kiros, "Hegemonic Ideology and Counter Hegemonic Vision: An Analysis of the African Food Crisis" (paper presented at the annual meeting of the African Studies Association, Boston, 1983).

stratification, role differentiation, capital accumulation, high technology and bureaucratized institutions—were crucial to the development of modern nations.

Apter, in *The Politics of Modernization*, is quick to point out that political development or the absence of it is to be explained by the presence or absence of commercialization and industrialization respectively.[3] Commercialization and industrialization are, for Apter, political relationships in that they presuppose the availability of human personnel who engage in commerce and develop industries. Apter and others are, we might say, the technical thinkers who appropriate the economy by nurturing the requisite business and technical acumen in the field of material development. Apter implicitly advances the argument, against the theses of the dependency school, that the political (commercialization and industrialization) and the economic spheres are not strictly interdependent and that development is not determined by economic factors to the total exclusion of political determinants. Commercialization and industrialization, contends Apter, gain life and meaning as economic activities only if they are grounded upon modernizing institutions which glorify the technical thinkers as innovative minds.

I suggest that commercialization and industrialization are indeed important components of Africa's potential to develop materially but not until technically and morally responsible native Africans fully manage the continent's resources. Africans must be given a chance to become the technicians themselves.

In fact, Apter seems to argue that it is only when a nation is politically developed in the above sense (having the requisite thinkers and institutions, such as in the U.S.A.) that the nation becomes ready for material development. The sensitivity to the roles and interventions of class biases implicit in the visions of the innovators and in the priorities of the corresponding institutions— which are the themes of Marxian class analysis—are conspicuously absent from Apter's vision of development. For Apter's "marginal citizens" are scholars, bureaucrats, legislators, and technocrats who are trained at the center. According to Apter, these marginal

---

[3]David Apter, *The Politics of Modernization* (Chicago: The University of Chicago Press, 1965), 123-313.

citizens will contribute to the crucial creation of role differentiation, social stratification, and institutionalization of political life in
Africa.

In a similar vein, Riggs, in *Administration in Developing
Countries*, argues that agrarian societies are societies whose
institutions are nonspecialized or, as Parson's would have it,
societies with ascriptive norms, particularistic and diffuse
orientations, as opposed to the universalistic and specific
orientations of the developed world.[4]

In short, for these scholars, the phenomenon of underdevelopment, of which Africa is an example, for the most part is a
consequence of the absence of modernizing institutions. However,
if we ask these scholars why did economic and political development not occur in Africa to the extent that it did in the developed
nations, they might probably resort to racial, climatic, and cultural
factors as explanations, as Toynbee did before them. They are not
interested in pondering the question since the self-imposed task of
modernization theorists, such as Apter, is the description and
quantification of the empirical realities in the underdeveloped
nations. The silent premise in modernization theory seems to be
that modernization, thus the actuality of material development, is
an evolutionary process through which "all" nations are allowed
to travel but upon which only a few have managed to embark.

If the above question were put to David McClelland,
however, one might get the following discourse in the social/
psychological process of material development. The essentials of
McClelland's classic book, *The Achieving Society*, may be
summarized as follows. McClelland's premise is that whenever we
observe the absence of economic growth, we can safely infer that
there is material underdevelopment. Given the premise, he then
proceeds to formulate the major hypothesis that achievement
motivation is in part responsible for economic growth. Those
countries whose citizens have or develop the achievement
motivation grow, and thus become materially developed. The
fundamental problem of what achievement actually entails,
however, is largely ignored; namely, whether it is a historical

---

[4]Fred W. Riggs, *Administration in Developing Countries: the Theory
of Prismatic Society* (Boston: Houghton Mufflin, 1964), 200-37.

41

product which varies from generation to generation, or whether it is a uniform and standard network of values and aspirations that people pass on from generation to generation. Rather, achievement motive is treated as an ideal-type that is unchanged by time.

According to McClelland the capacity that persons might have to develop themselves economically is influenced significantly by the personality types they are or aspire to be. To Max Weber's credit, instructs McClelland, the personality types Protestantism carefully nurtured were precisely the ideal components of economic development that capitalism needed—namely, the self-reliant personalities who struggle to fulfill God's wish by diligently working and thus accumulating material wealth, thereby helping themselves without depending on anything else except their own intellect and labor. The presence of these personalities became the necessary condition for the birth of capitalism in Western Europe.

The diligent, competitive, profit-motivated, calculating, and aggressive human types, in short the capitalists, acquired these characteristics as a result of the influence of the Protestant ethic; as is well known, the above insight was Max Weber's central contribution to development literature. Religion in the particular form of Protestantism added the much-needed ideological incentive for the believers to be confident of themselves and what they could do to external nature with the conviction that God was there guiding their hands and directing their vision. The believers were convinced that the achievement motive was a God-infused aspiration to which they ought to devote themselves. According to McClelland, Protestantism (the spiritual incentive) and capitalism (the economic incentive) with all the necessary material requisites—capital, raw materials, and a laboring class—worked in a complementary fashion and rendered rational economic progress possible.

McClelland, closely following Weber, writes,

> The Protestant Reformation might have led to earlier independence and mastery training, which led to greater Achievement, which in turn led to the rise of modern capitalism. Certainly, Weber's description of the kind of personality type which the Protestant Reformation produced is startlingly similar to the picture we have drawn of a person with high achievement motivation. He notes that Protestant

working girls seemed to work harder and longer, that they saved their money for long-range goals, that Protestant entrepreneurs rose to the top more often in the business world despite the initial advantages of wealth many Catholic families on the Continent had. In particular, he points out that the early Calvinist businessman was prevented by his religious views from enjoying the results of his labor. He could not spend money on himself because of scruples about self-indulgence and display, and so, more often than not, he reinvested his profits in his business, which was one reason he prospered. What, then, drove him to such prodigious feats of business organization and development? Weber feels that such a man gets nothing out of his wealth for himself, except the irrational sense of having done his job well. This is exactly how we define the achievement motive in coding for it in fantasy.[5]

To the above insights of Weber, McClelland adds the further insight that

Protestantism also involved a revolt against excessive reliance on the institutional church. Luther preached the 'priesthood of all believers': the individual did not have to depend exclusively on more learned experts, but should read his Bible for himself and find guidance directly.... It seems very probable then that Protestant parents would stress earlier self-reliance and mastery of at least reading skills so that their children could fulfill their religious duties better. Such training, as we have seen, may well have increased the Achievement in the children.[6]

---

[5]David McClelland, *The Achieving Society* (Princeton: D. Van Nostrana Company, 1961), 47.

[6]McClelland, *The Achieving Society*, 48-49.

43

The tenets of Protestantism—self-reliance, relentless struggling to be chosen by God as the most deserving, an endless quest for self-improvement with perfection as the goal—gradually became the chief organizing principles of modern capitalism in practice. Those selected few, who had struggled to make it and thus become the successful modern entrepreneurs, enabled capitalism to become the most dominant mode of production in Europe. Economic growth coupled with industrialization became the concrete features of the developed world. These features buttressed by the spiritual force of the achievement motive commanded the good faith of modern men and women. The achievement motive, we might say, became the organizing principle of all developed nations. Clearly, the Protestant Reformation as a producer of achievement was basically a Western European phenomenon; so have McClelland and Weber before him argued.

We agree that the developed world is developed precisely because of the achievement motive. From this thesis, it is not too far drawn to advance the corollary thesis that the underdeveloped world is underdeveloped precisely because it lacked the achievement motivation, whereas in Western Europe, religion and capital seem to have founded an alliance with each other and, through this forged unity, managed to fuse the spiritual and material dimensions. In Africa, we hypothesize that we cannot point to such an effective unity of the spiritual and the material; for the most part these two dimensions of development seem to point toward parallel but never converging goals unlike what they did in Western Europe.

Thinking about the African situation and recalling the activities of the missionaries and their various attempts to Christianize Africa, we can ask why the achievement motive was not inculcated in the African citizens' minds? And, if it had been inculcated, what would the concrete results have been? Would Africa have undergone economic growth under the leadership of its diligent, God-fearing, and achievement-oriented populace? Did Africans resist the efforts of Protestant missionaries to inculcate the virtues of the Protestant ethic? If so, why? Why did Africans resist? Could we account for the resistance by studying pre-colonial and colonial Africans' view of themselves, their culture, and their religious systems? These are very fundamental and hard questions that might be put to McClelland, but we wonder if his psychological/historical framework is really equipped to answer them.

The Dependency School and Hegemonic Ideology

In a significant sense, Walter Rodney's theory of African underdevelopment easily may be construed as belonging to the dependency school. Rodney himself would not have objected strongly to the label. It is because of our view that Rodney is a dependency theorist that our review of the dependency school commences with a summary of his *How Europe Underdeveloped Africa*. The essentials of the book may be summarized as follows.

To the question: How did nations and whole continents—such as Africa—come to be differently developed in the first place? Rodney responded,

> One of the most difficult questions to answer is exactly why different peoples developed at different rates when left on their own. Part of the answer lies in the "superstructure" of human society. That is to say, as human beings battled with the material environment, they created forms of social relations, forms of government, patterns of behavior and systems of belief which together constituted the superstructure—which was never the same in any two societies. The religious belief that a certain forest was sacred was the kind of element in the superstructure that affected economic activity, since that forest would not be cleared for cultivation.[7]

From this remarkably insightful passage, we can draw at least two central propositions:

1.   A significant amount of the empirical phenomenon of Africa's material underdevelopment can be carefully explained through a dispassionate analysis of its religious beliefs and

---

[7]Walter Rodney, *How Europe Underdeveloped Africa* (Washington: Howard University Press, 1971), 9.

45

practice; or more broadly the phenomenon can be explained through an analysis of Africa's original and adopted culture. We shall attempt to comment on this proposition later in this chapter; it suffices here to mention that Rodney was aware of the hegemony and ideology view although he does not use the terms in the way we do

2. To a considerable extent, underdevelopment as such—the African case is a living example—is influenced, conditioned, and sometimes even "determined" by environmental (natural and societal) factors. Of course, African men and women continue to struggle with the environment so as to overcome it; so far, however, they have not succeeded, and underdevelopment remains an integral part of the African human condition

For the most part, Rodney's book concentrates more on the second proposition than the first.

It is Rodney's chief contention that Africa is materially underdeveloped because of the following:

1. Africa's economy was systematically plundered through the violence of the slave trade that dismantled the crafts-oriented economy and in its place imposed an export-oriented economy, in which an economy based on African needs (however rudimentary these needs might have been) was gradually replaced by a growth-oriented European economy that catered to the needs of the European slave traders

2. In East Africa and the Sudan, Arabs also participated in the enslavement of Africans and plundered the continent's economy—that is, they accumulated money by selling African laborers to rich Arab merchants, who profiteered from cheap and often unpaid labor power. As Rodney put it, "African slaves in Arab hands became domestics, soldiers and agricultural serfs. Whatever surplus they produced was not for reinvestment and multiplication of capital, as in the West Indian or North American systems, but for consumption by the feudal elite"[8]

---

[8]Rodney, *How Europe*, 143.

3. The European industrial revolution, upon which the birth and maturity of capitalism depended, rendered necessary the coercion and systematic attempt at converting the rural African peasant from a self-sustaining producer of petty commodities into a paid and unpaid laborer for European industrialists, plantation owners, and slave owners. Historically speaking, slavery eventually led to colonialism. The quest for superindustrialization, the goal of Europe, meant the conquest of the modicum of freedom that the African peasant or African farmer had; in particular, the possibility of limited self-sufficiency, as in the precolonial period, became replaced by dependency upon Europe's needs—the industrialization and technologization of the remnants of Europe's agricultural spheres. As Rodney put it,

    > Industrialization does not only mean factories. Agriculture itself has been industrialized in capitalist and socialist countries by the intensive application of scientific principles to irrigation, fertilizers, tools, crop selection, stock breeding. The most decisive failure of colonialism in Africa was its failure to change the technology of agricultural production. The most convincing evidence as to the superficiality of the talk about colonialism having "modernized" Africa is the fact that the vast majority of Africans went into colonialism with a hoe and came out with a hoe. Some capitalist plantations introduced agricultural machinery, and the odd tractor found its way into the hands of African farmers; but the hoe remained the overwhelmingly dominant agricultural element[9]

4. The concrete result of the above factors is the living and noticeable fact of Africa's state of economic backwardness, capital-dependency, foreign aid dependency, and the neocolonial status of most formally independent nations.

---

[9]Rodney, *How Europe*, 219.

Rene Dumont has recently documented the existence of some of the empirical indices of material backwardness in his most recent work.[10] However, for Rodney, the existence of the indisputably true empirical indices of underdevelopment in Africa are really consequences of European and Arabian slave trades, European colonialism, and imperialism. Rodney said, "when the 'experts' from capitalist countries do not give a racist explanation, they nevertheless confuse the issue by giving as causes of underdevelopment the things which really are consequences."[11] In other words, insofar as causes and consequences have become reversed, we shall remain in the dark each time we reflect upon the phenomenon of underdevelopment

5. Imperialism too has played a decisive role in the prevention of the African productive forces from developing as the European productive forces did. Imperialism, by draining the indigenous wealth of Africa, made it impossible for Africa to develop

6. After colonialism became an unwise policy for European colonizers to pursue in that the quest for self-determination by the colonized became uncontrollable, the brutal and direct system of colonialism was replaced by psychological and indirect colonialism through the cultivation of some well-trained indigenous manipulators of the system. Africans thus begin to colonize themselves. The colonial apparatus was formally dismantled but the colonized mind seems to be living and living well. Rodney does not pursue the above theme rigorously, but he certainly had a perceptive insight into the operation of what we would like to call "colonialism through hegemonic ideas." Again, we shall pursue this theme later

A careful look at the six factors which we just summarized cannot help but lead us to the conclusion that Rodney tends to stress that the causes of African underdevelopment are for the

---

[10]Rene Dumont and Marie-France Mattin, *Stranglehold on Africa* (London: Andre Dutch, 1983).

[11]Rodney, *How Europe*, 22.

most part external; it is European and Arab slave owners, colonizers, and imperialists who are the human agents of underdevelopment. In a lucid passage, Rodney wrote that "the most profound reasons for the economic backwardness of a given African nation are not to be found inside the nation. All that we can find are the symptoms of underdevelopment and the secondary factors that make for poverty."[12] Passages such as this guide one to conclude that Rodney in many respects paved the way for the emergence of dependency theory. Perhaps a brief review of the works of Samir Amin, a well-known dependency theorist, will show the similarities between Rodney's concerns and Amin's.

Rodney shares with the dependency theorists the important premise that the causes of African underdevelopment are for the most part externally generated. Amin is a most prolific dependency theorist who seems to have given an elaborate and sophisticated analysis of Africa's dependency, and therefore its underdevelopment. He has been greatly influenced by Frank. For Frank, as for Amin, the primary determinants of development/ underdevelopment in the underdeveloped world are as follows:

1. The past and present unequal economic relationship between the developed and underdeveloped have the form of a metropolis (Great Britain) and satellite (Africa) relationship
2. All the present merchants, professionals, wealthy farmers, and small farmers are largely of European extraction, as, for example, in South Africa
3. The semiautonomous indigenous groups that coordinate European merchant, professional, and agricultural needs are the newly formed bourgeois
4. The present economic relationships between the metropolis and the satellite countries are marked by a chronic balance-of-payment deficit, a deficit which directly signifies dependency

For Frank and for Amin, these above determinants produce what Frank calls a dependency complex, characterized by a

---

[12]Rodney, *How Europe*, 22.

political/economic network called metropolis and satellite relationship. Finally, Frank, as Amin after him, stresses that colonialism, contrary to the thesis of modernization theorists, did not promote modernization or material development of the productive forces (capital and labor); on the contrary, the absence of modernization on a large scale in Africa leads one to assume the backwardness and the underdevelopment of the productive forces. In short, colonialism arrested the modernization process by indirectly preventing the development of real and independent productive forces.

Amin, in particular, is interested in explaining the material/economic causes of African underdevelopment or, what he prefers to call more broadly, the phenomenon of "unequal development." Whereas Frank analyzes the metropolis and satellite relationship, Amin analyzes the "center and periphery" relationship, in which the center is equivalent to the metropolis, and the satellite to the periphery. Unlike Frank, Amin tends to meld the political and the economic facts of underdevelopment in his center and periphery categories. Frank, on the other hand, tends to stress the political ramifications of underdevelopment with his category of metropolis/satellite relationships. Both of them, however, in a complementary fashion, consider the purely political (Frank's) and the conflicted economic and political (Amin's) dimensions as aspects of underdevelopment; both aspects are expressions of dependency. Since Amin's focus of research was Africa, we shall attempt to summarize the essentials of his dependency theory as applied to Africa. In his analysis of the center and periphery relationships, Amin advances and attempts to test the following propositions as the determinants of Africa's underdevelopment:

1. The Industrial Revolution in Europe was preceded by the agricultural revolution; the mechanization of agriculture and the consequent quest for cheap labor impelled the European modernizers to employ violence and force non-European African agrarian societies to transform the feudal or "natural" modes of production into modes of production subordinated to capital. In tropical Africa, for example, peasants were compelled to produce "compulsory crops" and then sell their labor power to the European-owned mines, factories, or plantations. This mode of production,

normally called "the colonial mode of production," was the first historical distortion of African economy. This distortion inevitably led to the gradual destruction of the peripheral African agrarian farmers' attempts at self-sustenance in that their petty commodities could not withstand the competition of commodities produced by those African farmers who had sold their labor power to European capitalist markets at the center

2. The process of industrialization that Europeans introduced into Africa after 1945 systematically made the African farmer a wage laborer for foreign-owned plantations and factories and, by paying the African laborer very low wages, the European owners of the means of production extracted high surplus profits from their capital investments. The concrete results of the colonial mode of production were high savings and investments for the European owners and lack of savings, the absence of investments, and the spirit of dependency for African farmers and wage workers alike

3. As industrialization accelerated, a new international division of labor set by the multinational corporations came into prominence. Under this new form of the international division of labor, the following economic relationships are extant: at the center, "software" (technological research facilities along with innovative thinkers and managers) is nurtured; at the periphery, as in Africa, "hardware" at extremely low wages is produced. Despite the adjective "multinational," Amin argues, the multinational firm is actually national in origin; its top management is American, Japanese, British, or German[13]. As Amin put it,

> The old division of labor, in which the underdeveloped countries supplied raw materials and the advanced countries supplied the manufactured goods is being replaced by a different division, in which the former

---

[13]Samir Amin, *Unequal Development* (New York: Monthly Review Press, 1976), 203-26.

supply the products and the manufactures, while the second supply the equipment and the "software"[14]

Clearly, this type of relationship reinforces the phenomenon of unequal development in that the developed industrial nations, by centralizing and retaining the technocratic knowledge which is necessary for mastery of the forces of production, obstruct the material progress of Africa; therefore, underdevelopment is the result. The particular effects of this phenomenon are as follows:

1. Insofar as technical knowledge is centralized, it will be distributed unevenly, thus perpetuating the need for technical/intellectual dependency on those who have such knowledge—the "multinational firms." Technical autonomy for Africa will thus be an impossibility. Imported experts will have to do the technical thinking for Africa

2. Concrete technical know-how, given its centralization, will not be obtainable easily by those at the periphery. When available, it will be too expensive to obtain

3. When a limited amount of technology is sent to Africa, it is concentrated in the cities of different regions of the continent; this phenomenon will gradually result in the development of the city and the underdevelopment of rural areas thus perpetuating center and periphery relationships. The relationship between the cities and the countryside will be distorted: for example, jobs may only be relatively available in the cities to which job-seeking farmers will flock without necessarily securing employment. The results are that the lands from which they came will be unproductive and that the cities will be overcrowded, thus leading to concentration of the urban poor on the one hand and uncultivated lands on the other

It is because of these center periphery dependencies that Africa is still underdeveloped, according to Amin.

---

[14]Amin, *Unequal Development*, 41-212.

The School of Political Economy and Hegemonic Ideology

One of the most systematic political/economic approaches to the study of African underdevelopment was undertaken by T. Szentes in his classic *The Political Economy of Underdevelopment*. Development for Szentes, like Rodney before him, presupposes the "dialectic" of quantitative and qualitative change of evolution and revolution; that is to say, any quantitative and qualitative development of the industrial world necessarily entails a quantitative and qualitative underdevelopment of the under-developed world. The underdevelopment of Africa is a constant reminder of the empirical fact of the dialectic of revolution and evolution. This particular insight leads Szentes to make this very important methodological point:

> In order to understand the State and historical development of the underdeveloped countries, it is necessary to understand the state and historical development of the whole world economy and society as well.[15]

In the extensive literature on the political economy of underdevelopment, statistical indices such as GNP and per capita income are employed as measures of a country's state of development. These indices, however, gloss over the conditions of production, distribution, and utilization of the national income. Thus a given GNP or a given per capita income, though very important as measures, captures only some of the empirically visible aspects of an otherwise complex dynamic of underdevelopment. The same problem of partial illumination is true of the inherently limited power of statistical indices as explanations; for example, statistical indices such as high population in agriculture, very little capital per head, low savings, backward agrarian techniques, high indebtedness, or old methods of production have a limited explanatory power. The same

---

[15]T. Szentes, *The Political Economy of Underdevelopment* (Budapest: Akademiai Kiado, 1973), 15; see also Amiya Kumar Bagchi, *The Political Economy of Underdevelopment* (Cambridge: Cambridge University Press, 1982).

explanatory limitation is evident in demographic indices: (a) high fertility rates; (b) high mortality rates and low life-expectancy at birth; (c) rudimentary hygiene, public health, and sanitation; and (d) rural overcrowding. Statistical indices of the cultural and political type, for example, illiteracy and rudimentary education, extensive prevalence of child labor, inferiority of women's status, and traditionally determined behavior for the bulk of the populace are also self-limiting in what they can explain. Finally, empirical technological visibles such as low yields per acre, no facilities for the training of technicians and engineers, inadequate and crude communication and transportation facilities, and crude technology tell us even less about the real causes of underdevelopment. If we were to seek an explanation of underdevelopment as such through the various possible permutations of the statistical indices, we would be caught in a static "vicious circle" that is well displayed in Figure 1.

This vicious circle of underdevelopment in Africa as a whole (with the exception of South Africa) has been well documented by theorists, agronomists, and economists. Goran Hyden has thus studied Tanzania; Samir Amin has investigated Northern and part of Western Africa; Rene Dumont and Marie-France Mattin have studied Nigeria; and Robert Bates has masterfully studied the political function of markets in the determination of agricultural policies in tropical Africa. I wish to analyze Bates' thesis at the end of the chapter below. But the indices of this vicious circle, argues Szentes, are really symptoms and consequences of, not causes of, underdevelopment. Though enumerating and identifying the indices is a necessary requisite from a scientific standpoint, the challenging task is to penetrate the indices themselves and ground them in either history or in a combination of history and political economy so as to search for the hidden causalities of those symptoms and consequences. When the indices are viewed from the standpoint of political economy as opposed to pure economics, their explanatory limitation (as opposed to their descriptive usefulness) becomes evident. We shall pursue these themes further in chapters 4 and 5 below.

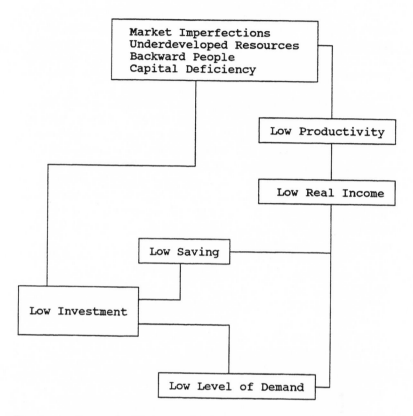

Fig. 1:   Szentes' Vicious Circle of Limiting Factors of Underdevelopment

Szentes' chief criticisms of a political economics approach to the study of underdevelopment may be summarized as follows:

1. Classifications of statistical indices cannot disclose the principal economic and social characteristics of underdevelopment

2. International obstacles—the "vicious circle" as we like to call them—are ahistorical attempts at an explanation of underdevelopment

3. Stages-of-growth theories such as Rostow's, which shares similar premises with the statistical indices approach, gloss

over and at times even explicitly disregard the historically generated essential differences of the conditions of production in the "developing" underdeveloped countries

For Szentes, the explanation of underdevelopment requires a historical and analytic approach that must start both historically and logically with the examination and evaluation of colonialism, the analysis of capitalist world economy and the international division of labor, and a critical study of "racism."

Furthermore, contrary to the premise of political economy which suggests that the causes of underdevelopment are internal factors that are unique to the underdeveloped countries themselves, Szentes thinks that the causes of underdevelopment are both internal and external and that even the internal factors may ultimately be consequences and symptoms of the external factors. Consider the following passage:

> The first step in establishing a colonial economy was the construction of transport and communications i.e., infrastructure . . . for transporting its products to the "mother" country. To be convinced that the construction of transport served the very purpose of colonial exploitation consciously and purposefully, it will suffice to look at the railway map of these countries. The railway lines, instead of connecting the various economic areas of the country in question, run between the sources of raw materials and the seaports handling their export to the metropolitan country.[16]

For Szentes, the experience of colonialism is one of the most central, if not the only, cause of underdevelopment, which historically led to the now-prevalent existence of internal factors. Consider his following passage: "The underutilization of natural resources, low labor productivity, etc., are symptoms and consequences rather than causes of backwardness."[17] Some of the most visible and "quantifiable" features of the externally

---

[16]Szentes, *Political Economy*, 118-19.

[17]Szentes, *Political Economy*, 125.

caused manifestations of "internal" backwardness which peasants have adopted are economic dependence on foreign capital, systematic income drain by foreign capital and various other forms of regular income losses in external relations, disintegrated economy with open character and deformed structures of branches, society where vast wealth exists along with massive poverty, and dependencies that are deeply rooted in the system of imperialism. There are at least four forms of these dependences: (a) direct dependence, such as a given country's mining sector's dependence on foreign capital—such as technology—to extract the minerals; (b) trade dependence, for example, a dependent country produces commodities and terms of trade for the industrial nation; (c) financial dependence, where the dependent country is at the mercy of the industrial nation's banking system and credit systems; and (d) technical dependence such that the industrial nation's experts, advisors, teachers, and agronomists are the sources of the indispensable technical knowledge which is systematically concentrated in the industrial countries' research centers.

In the course of time, these internal factors become integral aspects of the dependent countries' own institutions, thereby acquiring a momentum of their own. The internal factors, though, are products of colonial history divorced from traditional roots. Szentes speaks for himself: "the internal structure of the under-developed countries is not only the product of the penetration of external, international forces, but . . . this structure, once it has become established, will itself provide a basis for maintaining this penetration."[18] We will comment more extensively on this crucial passage in the final sections of the chapter; here, it will suffice to mention that the consolidation of this systematic penetration did provide a solid basis for the ongoing penetration of hegemonic political/economic ideas that serve the purpose of keeping African countries and leaders from developing any vision of how they can themselves develop their own nations, with a minimal involvement of the efforts of outsiders. Intellectual independence not only was considered subversive by colonial governments, but was systematically repressed by them. The intellectual dependencies that are

---

[18]Szentes, *Political Economy*, 230.

prevalent in Africa today are significantly conditioned by this past repression.

The political/economic approach has recently evolved into a rather engaging—albeit controversial—approach in the seminal book by Michael Lipton, *Why Poor People Stay Poor?* Lipton's chief thesis is as follows:

> The most important class conflict in the poor countries of the world today is not between labor and capital. Nor is it between foreign and national interests. It is between the rural classes and the urban classes. The rural sector contains most of the poverty, and most of the low-cost sources of potential advance; but the urban sector contains most of the articulateness, organization and power. So the urban classes have been able to "win" most of the rounds of the struggle with the countryside; but in so doing, they have made the development process needlessly slow and unfair. Scarce land, which might grow millets and bean sprouts for hungry villagers instead produces a trickle of costly calories from meat and milk, which few except the urban rich (who have ample protein anyway) can afford. Scarce investment, instead of going into water-pumps to grow rice, is wasted on urban motorways. Scarce human skills design and administer, not clear village wells and agricultural extension services, but world boxing championships in showpiece stadia. Resource allocations, within the city and the village as well as between them, reflect urban priorities rather than equity or efficiency. The damage has been increased by misguided ideological imports, liberal and Marxism, and by the town's success in buying off part of the rural elite, thus transferring most of the costs of the process to the rural poor.[19]

---

[19]Quoted in Nick Moore, "Political Economy and the Rural-Urban Divide, 1967-1981," in the *Journal of Development Studies* 20/3 (April 1984): 5-28. Quotation on p. 15.

From this central paragraph, Moore extracts the following seven propositions, which we summarize below.

1. Contrary to dependency theory, which sees the main explanations of underdevelopment as a whole in the center-periphery relations, Moore proposed that more adequate explanations are located in relationships that are internal to the countries
2. Countries can be clearly divided into rural (agricultural) and urban sectors
3. There are major conflicts of interest between these two sectors
4. The sectors are each internally divided into class categories whose interests may diverge and conflict
5. Groups designated by class and location appear as solid political sectors pursuing the group interest in politics
6. The urban sector is generally more successful in politics, but only through "buying" the rural elite in a system by keeping the landless peasant subdued
7. The resultant pattern of resource allocation is inefficient in terms of aggregate growth and inequitable to the rural poor[20]

Lipton himself has responded to his numerous critics, who accused him of seeking to apply his urban bias hypothesis to all postcolonial less-developed countries (LDCs) in spite of the critics' allegation that the hypothesis is "very Indian," with the counter-argument that the evidence of urban bias is much more acute in most African LDCs than in India, where urban bias diminished somewhat in the 1970s.

It is precisely Lipton's own direct and confident reference to Africa's underdevelopment that inspired and supported our selection of his urban bias hypothesis as a valid and fruitful illumination of Africa's present status of underdevelopment characterized by psychological dependency long after the physical disappearance of colonialism in its classical form. For Lipton, "in much of Francphone Africa, both colonialism and anti-colonialism

---

[20]Moore, "Political Economy," 15.

were overwhelmingly urban-led and rurally-extractive."[21] This general statement suggests that the modern forms of under-development can be traced to the hegemonic ideas of the indigenous leaders (largely urban), who at first gave their willing cooperation to the colonial master, thus contributing to the introduction and consolidation of colonialism, and who later became independence leaders decolonizing their nations from the foreign colonizers. Lipton's thesis seems to state that presently the urbanites are the new perpetuators of the expropriation of the poor and of peasants in particular. Colonial domination is replaced by urban domination of the rural sector.

It is safe to assume that Africa as a whole is still a peasant society and the urban-led modernization process is largely rurally extractive. With the exception of the brief but necessary periods of work for wages either in the plantations of the countryside or in the relatively few industries in the cities, the peasants are dependent upon the land for sustenance; but their contribution to the development of the land upon which they so much depend is limited by their conspicuous poverty. Poor African peasants in particular can contribute to material development only if they are equipped with material and nonmaterial resources: capital, seeds, fertilizers, medical facilities, and access to technical and scientific knowledge through properly nurtured local educational institutions.

But if it is true, as Lipton contends, that urban bias results in the misallocation to the cities of the material resources required by the rural periphery for its development, and if this misallocation results in affluence for a selected few urbanites, and the perpetuation of rural backwardness and poverty, then the causes of the present forms of underdevelopment are evident. For the most part, African underdevelopment can no longer be imputed to external factors; according to Lipton, the phenomenon is largely attributed to internal factors, of which urban bias very likely is a variable.

---

[21]Michael Lipton, "Urban Bias Revisited," in the *Journal of Development Studies* 20/3 (April 1984): 139-67. Reference on page 142.

By way of testing the validity of the urban bias theory in Africa, Radcliff, for example, has studied Tanzania.[22] In Tanzania, a country that not only is independent but is also attempting to be self-reliant, material underdevelopment is a dismal reality apparently perpetuated by the Tanzanian state in concert with the elites. This thesis is forcefully argued by Philip Raikes. In one of his key passages, he writes,

> Prices throughout the country are controlled by the state, which also has monopoly control of almost all primary agricultural marketing, through cooperatives and parastatal marketing agencies up to 1976, and since then, with the abolition of the cooperatives, through the latter alone. In addition to this, there are the standard forms of state intervention through investment in infrastructure, provision of agricultural and other credit, agricultural research and extension and the various controlling activities of a large and growing bureaucracy. Finally, the state has attempted to change the whole basis of agricultural production in the past few years by moving the rural population into nucleated villages for the improved provision of services and more effective control over the process of production.[23]

It is fair to conclude from the above passage that

1. The direct determinant of material underdevelopment in Tanzania is the socialist state itself; the socialist state has assumed the role of the previous colonial state. The face of

---

[22]Lipton, "Urban Bias Revisited," 142.

[23]Philip Raikes, "The State and the Peasantry in Tanzania," in *Rural Development: Theories of Peasant Economy and Agrarian Change*, ed. John Harriss (London: Hutchinson, 1982), 354. For a similar view that examines the evolution of the petite bourgeoisie in Kenya, see G. Kitching, *Class and Economic Change in Kenya* (New Haven: Yale University Press, 1980), especially 413-56.

the exploiters has changed: foreign exploiters are now replaced by indigenous ones

2. Unlike the Chayanovian thesis—which denies class formation, and which is a view inherited by Lipton—Raikes argues that there are definite classes in Tanzania, and that there are different class levels among the peasantry[24]

As stated, the state and its bureaucrats have a major responsibility for the absence of material development and for consequent regional inequalities. But some responsibility must also be assumed by the rich peasantry, who are now playing the role of colonial employers. Tanzania's rich peasants hire foreign migrant labor from Rwanda and Burundi to weed and harvest cotton at very low wages. This exploitative activity is done without the knowledge and control of the Tanzanian state, thereby reducing the power of the state to accumulate capital.

Furthermore, the Tanzanian government's official policy of the "Africanization of the bureaucracy" also created a separate, albeit an indigenous, African class that fed itself on the backs of the landless and desperate peasantry. The domestication of the source of the landless peasantry's despair does not seem to have helped much the state's goal of total development. On the contrary, the rich peasantry, in alliance with the indigenous bureaucracy, continue to contribute toward Tanzania's under-development in the postcolonial period. To complicate the problem further, while on the one hand, as was just noted, the rich peasantry's interests coincide with those of the indigenous bureaucracy, on the other hand, they also conflict with the indigenous bureaucracy. The final relationship of these two forces ultimately is a mixture of conflict and identity of interest.

On the one hand, the rich peasantry's practice of hiring migrant and indigenous poor peasantry's labors results in the extraction of surplus value, thus the accumulation of capital to the detriment of the Tanzanian state, and sets its interests in conflict with those of the urban class. To the extent that the rich peasantry's and the urban wealthy classes' vision and practice of material development coincide through the process of the

---

[24]Raikes, "The State," 355.

exploitation of migrant and poor peasantry's labors, their goals interpenetrate and are the same.

In the end, within the larger context of the role and function of the world market, the conflicting and identical interests of the rich peasantry and the indigenous urban class restrict Tanzania's national agenda. Tanzania's priorities, which at times demand that the urban class independently develop and thus create a possible conflict of interests with foreign capitalists, are ultimately subordinated to international capital and the force of the world market. As Raikes argues, international capital has similar and specific requirements for export crops and for production processes which allow the maximum degree of control by capitalists through technical subordination of the laborers. He concludes that the identical and conflicting interests of Tanzania's rich peasantry and its urban class within the framework of an established world market necessarily imply the gradual emergence of a rich peasantry that not only has alliance with Lipton's urban class but itself constitutes a capitalist class of farmers. Raikes' chief conclusion by way of answering Lipton's followers, for whom class is not important, is that there are classes in agrarian societies which have their own modes of production different from the capitalist mode of production.[25]

The underdevelopment of Tanzania, according to Raikes, is to be explained by the existence in Tanzania of (a) planters/land owners, (b) an insensitive class of bureaucrats, and (c) the subordination of peasants and those bureaucrats to capital. If it is true that technology is necessary for the development of the productive forces, if it is true that capital is required for the purchase of technology from the industrial world, and if it is true that it is only the rich peasantry and the equally rich subsidy-giving state that could give technological aid to the poor peasantry, then it follows that the Tanzanian economy will remain underdeveloped without the spirited participation of its backbone—the poor peasantry.

The landless peasants—who seem to be aware of their double exploitation by capital both indigenous and foreign and by Tanzanian socialism—are resistant to suggestions from extension

---

[25]Raikes, "The State," 357.

advisors and developers. In so much that has been written by anthropologists and sociologists, peasant resistance to change has been treated as indicative of the peasantry's irrational mind. Lipton has effectively countered the above established argument with the following insightful argument. The poor peasantry's seeming irrationality is actually rational if only peasant behavior could be properly understood before it is judged. Peasants, Lipton contends, always decide under uncertainty—the uncertainty of the weather, the production of goods and the fluctuation of prices.[26] Given this changing reality, the poor peasantry, unlike the great "risk-taking" capitalist entrepreneurs, choose to produce less and somehow subsist without either gaining too much or losing too much.   They are astute economic calculators for whom profit maximization through risk-taking is not the main principle.

As G. Williams put the matter,

> Peasants resist outsiders' plans to change the countryside not out of an obtuse conservatism, but because of a clear and comprehensible preference for a way of life which allows them the freedom to manage their own resources. They will not welcome schemes for cooperation without clear evidence that the schemes will bring material benefits and improve their way of life, rather than destroy it.[27]

The poor peasants in particular seem to be aware in their own "provincial and suspicious" way that the various development packages handed to them in their respective nations—Nigeria, Kenya, the Sudan, Tanzania, and Ethiopia—are really not geared toward their interests: subsistence, integrated and stable commodity prices, improved education and medical care, and above all certainty and a stable world.   From the peasant's standpoint, the plans of urban modernization experts are irrelevant; they are systematic tricks for destabilizing the poor

---

[26]Michael Lipton, "Game Against Nature: Theories of Peasant Decision-making," in *Rural Development*, ed. John Harris, 259-68.

[27]G. Williams, "Taking the Part of Peasants," in *Rural Development*, ed. John Harris, 389.

peasant's world. The peasants respond to modernization and its advocates through the peasant's mode of politics, which is the world of "witch-craft accusations, or campaigns for the removal of particular individuals from office, with the support of their rivals among the local elite. Objectionable state directives are met by various strategies, from sullen obedience and a formal show of cooperation to dumb insolence."[28] Lipton draws our attention to the subtle ways peasants employ to resist the great schemes of systematic exploitation by those who come to develop them.

The peasants' refusal to contribute to their material development of their respective nations is anchored upon not merely conservatism or irrationality or the will not to change, but simply upon the view that the state, whether it is socialist or capitalist, is alien to them. The peasant thinks that the state belongs to the rich plantation owners and the city sophisticates. The peasants have negative opinions of what the state could do for them. The landless peasants in particular and the middle peasantry in general do not view themselves as integral citizens of their various states. The peasants seem to view the state as an encroachment upon their perceived freedom, as a hostile influence that has no respect for their intelligence, their experience, their little world of land, seeds, and oxen.

Now that we have dealt with the views of the different schools on the causes of Africa's underdevelopment, we now may outline our own reflections on the subject of Africa's underdevelopment.

Hegemony, Ideology, and Africa's Underdevelopment

Africa's underdevelopment is significantly influenced by ideologies—hegemonic religious, political/economic, and philo-sophical/moral norms. Africans held these ideas themselves during the precolonial period, the colonial period, and still do today. The basic idea is the view that humankind are influenced not only by material/economic incentives but also by ideas. We advance our theses in the form of a number of hypotheses. First we shall examine the following concepts: Rodney's thesis of dependency,

---

[28]Williams, "Taking the Part," 393.

political economy, the self in Africa, McClelland's concept of achievement and its relevance to Africa's material under-development, Gramsci's concept of culture and Africa's self-understanding, and some of the thoughts of Adam Smith.

The Idea of Dependency

I have three objections to Rodney's thesis. One is the lesson which students of African underdevelopment learn from Rodney: that the precolonial African mode of production was brutally destroyed by Europeans for the sake of the accumulation of capital by the Europeans. Rodney fails to distinguish consistently between the average European and the European owners of capital.

Another is that Rodney is misleading when he reduces the multiplicity of the causes of African underdevelopment to external factors, ignoring any internal factors which might have contributed or facilitated the penetration of the external factors. Rodney only hints at the role of the indigenous African accomplice. He refrains from asking the obvious question: Why did Africans succumb to the destructive ideology of a dependency mode of production thrust upon them at gunpoint?

Furthermore, Rodney's insights into the process of dependency are relevant only insofar as they illuminate underdevelopment in preindependence Africa; Africa's present economic reality is much more subtle and complicated than was the explicit dependency relationship between European colonialists and Africans. Africa still suffers from intellectual dependency.

The Hidden Ideas of Political Economy

The psychology of dependence is particularly evident in the ideology of political economy which holds sway over the minds and actions of African policy makers. Szentes among others forcefully argued this thesis, as was demonstrated earlier in this chapter. Central to the various views of political economists is the opinion that in one way or another, the underdevelopment of Africa was directly influenced by the priorities of the slave and colonial modes of production, to which the African peasant producer was systematically subjected. The peasants succumbed to these exploitative practices. In the beginning, argue the political economists, it was force which compelled Africans to yield their autonomy to the slave masters, the colonialists, and the capitalists; later it was material comfort experienced by few Africans, rich plantation owners, and bureaucrats which continued the domination. The state, the courts, and the police introduced a world view accompanied by force; the missionaries, colonial teachers, disseminated hegemonic ideas to civil society (churches, clubs, schools, universities, or research institutions) through a relentless effort at consensus formation. This theme leads us to an analysis of the formation of the self in its moral and cultural aspects.

The Self in Africa

Political economy points out that super material advantages for profit maximizers such as slave owners, colonial entrepreneurs, and owners of the means of production, backed up by guns, account for the penetration of foreign domination into Africa. At the same time, however, political economy does not reflect upon the central question: What must have been the conditions or the state of mind of the African natives when they yielded their autonomy to foreign domination? How did African men and women conceive of themselves as persons? A complete analysis of these questions would take us into the realms of anthropology, religion and moral philosophy. Below we will simply advance propositions which have yet to be fully tested to illuminate the moral/religious environment that must have contributed to foreign domination.

One's view of oneself largely influences the views and expectations that one has of others. If one views oneself as moral and religious, one is likely to expect others to be moral and religious as well. Furthermore, when the self is viewed within such a moral/religious framework, the meaning of morality and religion is largely assumed; and it is precisely such assumptions that define the nature of the problems that arose when the moral European confronted the moral African in the absence of a universally accessible interpretation of morality that would be common to all members of humankind, on the basis of which the first encounters between Africans and non-Africans could be understood by each other. It was not unreasonable on the part of

67

Africans to assume that the strangers, whether Arab or European, were moral/religious beings who under no circumstances would do Africans harm. If the African regarded himself/herself as moral and religious, it is probable that when slavery was introduced into the continent, Africans were taken by surprise; they must have been unprepared for the power of fate because they expected the moral/religious strangers to treat them as human beings worthy of respect. False or unreflective expectations, such as those of the African, are just as hazardous as a complete or self-righteous confidence in one's own power and ability to discount and undermine the power of others. In the Africans, it appears the latter was lacking.

If we look at Africans from the standpoint of the slave owners and colonizers we arrive at erroneous expectations of African behavior based on European morality. The European came to the Dark Continent to fulfill a self-imposed mission of exploration and adventure in the discovery of Africa, the extraction of its minerals, and the civilizing of its inhabitants. These missions were guided by the will of God in the eyes of some Europeans. For these Europeans, to be moral and religious meant to engage in the expropriation of the riches of nature and to materially develop oneself through hard work and the accumulation of wealth.

To the European explorer, the first African encountered must have been viewed as either an obstacle which stood in the way of appropriating nature, or a potential collaborator—the means through which he could appropriate nature. Historical documents indicate that the explorers chose the latter; they found Africans who yielded their autonomy to superior physical power as well as hegemonic ideas. The first encounter thus was an encounter of two moral beings whose moral assumptions were grounded upon different views and indeed different expectations, which were fulfilled for the Europeans and dashed for the Africans.

The African's anticipative moral power was too weak; it was assumptive and presumptive. The African moral individual captured only the positive aspect of morality; it failed to anticipate morality's negative power in the elementary and rudimentary stages of early capitalism. On a moral/religious plane, the conflict between the African and the non-African moralities may be reduced to this: Africans wanted to treat others and to be treated by others as autonomous human beings. The European assumed that to be moral did not preclude the possibility of using others as a means for achieving the material appropriation of the world. We shall return to this theme in the section on McClelland's Weberian conception of the achievement motive.

McClelland's Concept of Achievement and Its Relevance to Africa

Earlier we constructed a hypothetical first meeting between the European explorers and Africans. Although a universal standard theoretically was accessible to the moral beings in their first encounter, it was interpreted differently by each. The clash of different interpretations resulted first in slavery, then colonialism, and finally colonization by ideas, or what we call "psychological colonialism" by hegemonic ideas. To the moral dimension we now add an economic dimension borrowed from McClelland's insightful hypothesis of the achievement motivation.

Following Weber, McClelland argued that central to the possibility of material development is the principle of the achievement motivation. Given the achievement motivation, he argues, and given a capitalist ethos grounded upon the Protestant ethic, and given further a willing and acting subject whose goal is material and concomitant spiritual development, economic growth toward a technological civilization became historically possible in Western Europe. Those human beings who were willing to commit themselves to the achievement motive would become materially and spiritually developed.

In the hypothetical encounter the Africans seem not to have possessed the achievement motivation, focused as it is on winning. The Africans do not believe that a happy afterlife is necessarily won by the morally and economically best, but rather achieved by helping and caring for others, by reciprocity in a community of equals. Furthermore, traditionally for Africans, the possibility of material development from the standpoint of a community of equals does not stress what individuals can do by themselves; instead what the individual can or cannot do is integrally bound up with the views of and expectations from the assumed moral community of equals. The implicit assumption of individuals is that A, a given individual, lives within B, a moral community of equals that holds the same basic views, and that anything that A does will

69

be reciprocated by the other members of B. The Europeans, on the other hand, sought to contribute to their moral community not through "the community of equals" but through an individual's effort to advance himself economically and morally; the community would profit by the sum total of the wealth of individuals. For the Europeans, to advance oneself is to advance the community as a whole, because one is part of the community, and any advancement of a part is an advancement of the whole. It apparently did not occur to the Europeans that individuals might benefit at one another's expense rather than mutually helping one another. Furthermore, the particular whole was limited to the Christian community within European geopolitical borders. The possibility of allowing the Africans to become new members of the Christian community is dependent upon converting the African, and that inevitably required the colonization of Africa. The African could not be accepted as a responsible, autonomous, and mature individual. Consequently, God charged the Europeans to take care of the helpless, childlike African, by colonizing them.

If Weber and McClelland are right, material development was rendered possible by the injection of economic incentives into moral discourse and the injection of moral incentives into economic life. The moral and economic were reconciled systematically through what we would call the power of hegemonic ideology emanating from the material needs of human beings but ultimately grounded upon human beings' disposition to be moved by moral, ethical, and religious ideas. The powerful ideas of the Protestant ethic were not available in the moral world of the African; on the contrary it seems that material achievement was not regarded as the route to heaven. If our descriptions are correct, then the following points may be advanced:

1. The African moral world did not have a systematically developed political economy upon which it grounded its rich moral premise of life: that is, each person is charged with the responsibility to help and care for others

2. Some African Christian societies, such as those in Ethiopia, were particularly insensitive to the achievement motive; instead the Ethiopian version of Christianity emphasized that if one's material achievement was gained at the expense of material underachievement of others, the one has sinned. If

a hegemonic ideology such as the achievement motive had been internalized by the African, perhaps the initial encounter with the European would have taken a different turn. It would be impossible to say that an achievement-oriented African would have been powerful enough to withstand the force of the guns, but Africans would have been prepared to counter what they considered as moral evils of slavery and colonialism. Realistic and intelligent moral Africans would have been more difficult for the Europeans to colonize. Sometimes human beings tend to respect those who are realistic and intelligent more than those who are dreamy, compassionate, caring, and unable to say "no"

3. The precolonial kingdoms of Africa and their "glorious" virtues might not have had organizing principles of the later Protestant ethic type; their moral values must have been different thus accounting for their self-sufficient but not profligate development before their penetration by non-African peoples

The complex combination of these factors might provide a clue to the present phenomenon of material underdevelopment and the greater development of Western Europe compared to Africa. The Europeans were propelled by the achievement motive justified by the Protestant ethic and used the labor of colonized Africans. Given the internalized sets of moral premises that characterized African morality, the African must have been unprepared to face up to the challenge of history—the confrontation of their morality with an alien morality, one backed up by armed force. These points are intended to serve as an attempt to reconstruct the African past so as to understand present and future trends.

It should be underscored that the achievement motive is praiseworthy because it has contributed to material development; its absence from the African psychological makeup accounts for the lingering facts of hunger, malnutrition, and massive poverty, which are evidence of unrestrained material underdevelopment. The economic virtues of the Protestant ethic are not beyond criticism. One can justly argue that moral attributes such as recprocity—which we indicated might have been the dominant moral ideal of the African—are infinitely superior to cutthroat individualism. Reciprocity has the capacity to cement a bond, a sense of family among the members of a community of equals provided that all members of a community have the same interpretation of morality.

As was noted above, however, if a given person strongly believes in individual self-sufficiency and another person believes in reciprocity, and if political society composed of self-sufficient individuals is already materially developed and the community of reciprocity adherents is materially underdeveloped, any demand which the latter community would make from the former would be disregarded. In such a situation, what might be prudent to the community of reciprocity adherents is to assimilate for pragmatic reasons some of the virtues of developed political society. Rather than seeking charity and international aid, self-help should be the new norm for members of the African community, however difficult this might be given the long history of dependence. People then would respect the African community as a possessor of moral ideals: care, compassion, forgiveness, and judiciousness.

Gramsci's Concept of Culture and
Africa's Self-Understanding

We shall introduce this section with a relevant quotation on the concept of culture from the ideas of Gramsci:

> Culture is . . . organization, discipline of one's inner self, a coming to terms with one's own personality; it is the attainment of a higher awareness, with the aid of which one succeeds in understanding one's own historical value, one's own function in life, one's own rights and obligation. But none of these can come about through spontaneous evolution, through a series of actions and reactions which are independent of one's own will—as is the case in the animal and vegetable kingdoms, where every unit is selected and specifies its own organs unconsciously through a fatalistic natural law. Above all, man is mind, i.e., he is a product of history, not nature. Otherwise, how could one explain the fact, given that there have always been exploiters and exploited, creators of wealth and its

selfish consumers, that socialism has not yet come into being? The fact is that only by degrees, one stage at a time, has humanity acquired consciousness of its own value and won for itself the right to throw off the patterns of organization imposed on it by minorities at a previous period in history.[29]

The central concepts which I shall borrow from Gramsci's conception of culture are (1) self-organization through a self-willed discipline, (2) self-imposed obligation and an understanding of one's rights, (3) historical consciousness, and (4) the human being as mind and will, rather than matter. These concepts are relevant to the understanding of the externally imposed and self-incurred processes of African underdevelopment. Our comments below will be brief and shall be treated in more detail in the next chapter.

The African past during the precolonial period was not well organized; Africans were at a stage of self-discovery: the discovery of agrarian techniques and technologies; the discovery of the self through a mystical and quasi-religious interpretation of the African environment; the search for a proper place for the individual independent of his or her family, group, and village; the assessment of the power and capacities of the individual; the uncritical acceptance of the powers of chiefs, landlords, village priests, fathers, and mothers. All these factors added up to what we may call the organization of the community through the will of the real and imagined powers and rights of rulers from the level of the family to that of the village. African communities at that time must not have had a carefully worked out conception of the individual as spontaneous and capable of self-discipline.

For the most part, the African community in the precolonial time was a place into which individuals were coerced and systematically socialized by the power of the group. At least on a superficial level, the act rather than the spirit of participation was needed in the life of the community. Consequently it was difficult, if indeed possible, for an individual to develop into a confident, reflective, and self-disciplined person. In this sense the African did

---

[29]Antonio Gramsci, *Selections from Political Writings: 1910-20*, ed. Quintin Hoare (New York: International Publishers, 1977), 11.

73

not satisfy the minimal Gramscian requirement of a cultured human being and does not today.

If the element of self-organization through a self-willed discipline is lacking, the element of self-obligation and an understanding of one's own rights is equally inaccessible to the African. If the African was not encouraged to determine his or her destiny through trials and failures, then such a person would be unable to develop the capacities to be moral, to be rational, to endure pain and rejoice in the possibility of overcoming it, to construct utopias, and to interpret history with vision.

Instead, any individual who is prevented from participating in the choosing of the rights and obligations which he or she would assume as a member of a community cannot possibly assume them, as was briefly discussed in the previous example of the alienated Tanzanian peasant. Self-assumed obligations and rights are replaced by externally imposed obligations whether precolonial, or familial and state-imposed as at present. The African precolonial past and the postcolonial present are not particularly nurturing in the education of citizens toward intellectual and moral independence.

It is prudent for the African to acquire a historical as well as a natural and conventional understanding of Africa's present state of material underdevelopment. It is not an accident of nature. A naturalistic interpretation of underdevelopment would simply regard the phenomenon as God's will. By contrast, a historical interpretation would attempt to locate the multiple causes of underdevelopment in the needs of the capitalist mode of production of which the rich African classes were beneficiaries and the poor African peasants were and continue to be victims. The historical dimension of Africa's past and present ought to be made accessible to modern Africans so that they can construct their future. If this is done, then the development of Gramsci's cultured individual would have satisfied his third minimal requirement—historical consciousness.

A Final Theory of Underdevelopment
Found in Classical Political Economy

The Classical Political Economy of Adam Smith. According to the classical political economy of Adam Smith, central to a human being's existence is his or her healthy capacity for engaging in labor producing goods for direct use and for exchange. Smith hypothesized that by engaging in labor, humankind produces commodities for a "rude" market where the exchange values of the commodities are measured by the amount of toil and trouble required to produce them.

> It was not by gold or by silver, but by labor, that all the wealth of the world was originally purchased; and its value, to those who possess it, and who want to exchange it for some new productions, is precisely equal to the quantity of labor which it can enable them to purchase or command.[30]

Furthermore,

> though labor be the real measure of the exchangeable value of all commodities, it is not that by which their value is commonly estimated. It is often difficult to ascertain the proportion between two different quantities of labor. The time spent in two different sorts of work will not always alone determine this proportion. The different degrees of hardship endured and of ingenuity exercised must likewise be taken into account. There may be more labor in an hour's hard work than in two hours' easy business; or in an hour's application to a trade which it cost ten years' labor to learn than in a month's industry at any ordinary and obvious employment. But it is not easy to find any accurate measure either of hardship or ingenuity. In exchanging, indeed, the different productions of

---

[30]Adam Smith, *The Wealth of Nations* (Pelican Classics: London, 1974), 133.

different sorts of labor for one another, some allowance is commonly made for both. It is adjusted, however, not by any accurate measure, but by the haggling and bargaining of the market, according to that sort of rough equality which, though not exact is sufficient for the business of common life.[31]

These ideas are the essence of Smith's principles of economics, in which labor combined with demand and supply (haggling and bargaining) function as the economic organizers of any human society.

Smith elaborated these principles with the concept of the division of labor and the division of society into classes. Labor, claimed Smith, becomes considerably more efficient when it is compartmentalized or divided into immediately separable but ultimately combinable parts. In such a division of labor, a single task such as making a pin is performed by a number of laborers where

> one man draws out the wire, another straightens it, a third cuts it, a fourth points it, a fifth grinds it at the top for receiving the head; to make the head requires three distinct operations, to put it on is a peculiar business, to whiten the pins is another; it is even a trade by itself to put them into the paper; and the important business of making a pin is divided into about eighteen distinct operations, which in some manufactories, are all performed by distinct hands, though in others the same man will sometimes perform two or three of them.[32]

This highly divided mode of labor, said Smith, is infinitely superior to the earlier mode of the "rude society," where labor was undivided, and completion of a finished product was more time-consuming. The many advantages brought about by the theory of division of labor—saving of time, increase of labor efficiency, and

---

[31]Smith, *Wealth*, 134.

[32]Smith, *Wealth*, 134.

the invention of better machines—are a necessary although, says Smith, gradual consequence of a certain "propensity in human nature which has in view no such extensive utility"; and that propensity is "the propensity to truck, barter, and exchange one thing for another."[33]

It is crucial for the understanding of the theme of this book—the relationship of morality, political economy, and the human condition in Africa—that we keep in mind Smith's conception of the human not only as a laboring being but as a being who labors with the goals of trucking, bartering, and exchanging. As humans engage in laboring, their chief goal, claims Smith, is their own self-interest which a priori makes it difficult for them to consider the interests of others. Smith speaks for himself:

> It is not from the benevolence of the butcher, the brewer, or the baker that we expect our dinner, but from their regard to their own interest. We address ourselves, not to their humanity but to their self-love, and never talk to them of our own necessities but of their advantages.[34]

Smith's vision of the well-functioning economy is analogous to his theory of the division of labor motivated by self-interest. For Smith, the modern economy is divided into different classes with different talents; and with correspondingly different capacities. Each class would be expected to perform a single task well, and the ultimate combination of these tasks would yield a well-coordinated economic whole. This whole is Smith's model of the perfect society, a society with an interpenetrating set of well-functioning parts such as the systematic division of labor in making a pin.

Smith's economic society is composed of roughly three classes: capitalists, landlords, and laborers; each of these classes expects a different reward for its contribution to the whole. Thus, the capitalists contribute their capital in order to obtain maximal profit, the landlords receive money for the lands that they rent,

---

[33]Smith, *Wealth*, 113.

[34]Smith, *Wealth*, 118.

and workers obtain wages for their labor. Each class carries out its assigned task and in due time earns its corresponding rewards. In Smith's model economics, profit, rent, and wages are the organizing principles of economic conduct. In his economic analysis, capital sets the laboring process in motion; the capitalist invests in a given sector, thus opening employment prospects for laborers. Capital is to labor as gas is to the car, activating labor from an otherwise passive existence. The capitalist does not invest his or her capital from either compassion toward the laborers or patriotism toward society. The capitalist's motive for igniting the labor process (and thus rendering possible the wealth of a nation) is personal profit. Smith wrote as follows:

> It seldom happens that the person who tills the ground has wherewithal to maintain himself till he reaps the harvest. His maintenance is generally advanced to him from the stock of a master, the farmer who employs him, and who would have no interest to employ him, unless he was to share in the produce of his labor, or unless his stock was to be replaced to him with a profit. What are the common wages of labor depends everywhere upon the contract usually made between those two parties, whose interests are by no means the same. The workmen desire to get as much, the masters to give us little as possible. The former are disposed to combine in order to raise the wages of labor above their actual rate.[35]

Smith is describing a machine in a perfect balance. He seemed to be unaware of the economic domination of the masters, who own the means of production, over those who labor in order to obtain food. Smith was equally silent about the genealogy of that domination. As an analyst of the human condition under which the masters and laborers interact, Smith seemed to be more interested in describing the workings of the complex economic whole than in deciphering its genealogy or analyzing its hegemonic ideas.

---

[35]Smith, *Wealth*, 120.

It should be emphasized that for Smith the value of any human being to a society is essentially economic, estimated according to the person's capacity to engage in productive labor which in turn produces capital. The accumulation of capital is the key to a society's economic growth. Therefore, contends Smith, labor is useful only if the laborer uses commodities which humans can use (such as water and air) and which also are exchangeable for money, the accumulation of which produces capital which may give us "the Wretched of the Earth."

Furthermore, for Smith, labor is the essence and the source of all human values. It is from the effects of labor that material civilization is born. However, not all labor is the same; some is productive of capital, say cotton manufacturing, whereas Smith's famous example of a musician's trade from the standpoint of capital is unproductive. Productive labor is rewarded with wages, and capitalists with profit. Moreover, that capitalists contribute to the production of capital, which is physically produced by the laborer, presents a crucial problem which Smith struggles to solve: namely, how are prices determined?

This problem was easily solved in Smith's rude society. Smith writes,

> In that early and rude state of society which precedes both the accumulation of stock and the appropriation of land, the proportion between the quantities of labor necessary for acquiring different objects seems to be the only circumstance which can afford any rule for exchanging them for one another. If among a nation of hunters, for example, it usually costs twice the labor to kill a beaver which it does to kill a deer, one beaver should naturally exchange for or be worth two deer. It is natural that what is usually the produce of two days' or two hours' labor, should be worth double of what is usually the produce of one day's or one hour's labor. If the one species of labor should be more severe than the other, some allowance will naturally be made for this superior hardship; and the produce of

one hour's labor in the one may frequently exchange for that of two hours labor in the other.[36]

Ancient societies did have elaborate mechanisms of exchanging goods. Bartering was one such mechanism; goods were exchanged with one another relative to labor they embodied. Many African nations still participate in such bartering. In Africa as well as in many other so-called rude societies, goods are deemed valuable if they are found useful for human survival. Goods are not useful just because they can be exchanged for money. For Smith, however, societies that do not exchange values are simply primitive.

Smith's rude society had a rather simple solution to the problem of pricing: that is by directly exchanging commodities using an estimation of the labor time and the hardship involved in obtaining the commodities to establish their relative values. To the determination of price in the manufacturing society of his own day, Smith adds further components to the picture, namely the principles of profit, wages, and rent; the introduction of machinery to alleviate the hardships of labor; and the division of labor to cut down production time. In Smith's manufacturing society, a given commodity is not wholly owned by one laborer as in the rude society; rather, the ownership is shared by the capitalist, the landlord, and the laborer.

The natural commodity in the manufacturing society, Smith seems to contend, is the sum total of labor time and toil, as adjusted by machine and division of labor, and profit, wages, and rent. There are two kinds of price though, says Smith: natural price and market price. Natural price is neither more nor less than what is sufficient to pay the rent for the land, the wages of the laborer, and the profits of the capitalist who provided the initial financing.[37] Market price is the actual price at which a commodity is sold; this form of price is determined by the laws of the market, and may or may not be above the natural price; the

---

[36]Smith, *Wealth*, 150.

[37]Smith, *Wealth*, 158.

adjusts to the law of supply and demand.[38] In the rude society, he reminds us, prices were determined by a process of bartering which took into consideration both the time and effort required to produce each commodity. Finally, Smith makes the more crucial distinction between the economy of a rude society and that of a modern society.

In the modern economy, he points out, commodities are exchanged for money, which is used to purchase other commodities, which are in turn sold for money. Value is then measured by money. Money, for Smith, is an objective measure. Smith seemed unaware that money is a commodity as any other commodity. The rude society did not use money since it worked through the direct exchange of commodities.

Smith answered the question, How is the price of a commodity determined in a modern economy? Labor is the source of all economic value; commodities are the products of labor; commodities have different exchange values. In a rude society, selective values of commodities are directly negotiated by the producers; in a modern economy, commodities are not exchanged for each other, but are bought and sold for money. The market price is the measure of a given commodity's market's worth, which reflects labor time, toil, investment of capital, and the pressures of supply and demand. This is how Smith explained the determination of price in his *The Wealth of Nations*.[39]

In precolonial Africa, which could serve as an example of Smith's rude society, money was not a commodity, but a crude measure that served as an equalizer of goods destined for reciprocal usage. Goods were often directly exchanged for goods, and money was used to facilitate the reciprocal exchange. Profit was not the commanding principle of the precolonial African economy.

In summary, Smith's understanding of modern economic society is that the whole is composed of interdependent parts, parts consisting of three classes (capitalists, landlords, and

---

[38]Smith, *Wealth*, 159-67.

[39]For a remarkably lucid exposition of Smith's economic theory as a whole, see Ronald Meek, *Precursors of Adam Smith* (London: Dent, 1973).

laborers) with different but ultimately intertwined goals. The modern economy encourages that spirit of competition. Individuals, through dexterity, imagination, and thrift, try to better their material life. Under the laws of demand and supply, competitive individuals work inventively and equilibrium is the result. When clashes arise, government, as a moral agent, intervenes and returns the economy to equilibrium, which is a necessary condition for the free and harmonious operation of the laws of supply and demand. Government intervention should be minimal, he warns, except in the public-oriented areas of the construction of harbors, canals, bridges, and highways, where Smith sees efficiency as the rule.[40]

A person does not choose to belong to a class; he or she is born to it. Furthermore, classes are not naturally reproduced. They are created by the intervention of powerful states and statesmen. In Africa, as dependency theorists argue, the center (industrial technological societies in north America, Europe, and Japan) and the periphery (the underdeveloped world in Africa, Asia, and Latin America) have been systematically plundering the labor and wealth of the various African nations by forcing individuals to belong to classes. The various classes in turn have been reproducing inequalities of wealth, power, access to resources, standards of living, educational opportunities, and upward mobility. The existence of classes continues to be legitimized through uncontested hegemonic ideas. The classes endorsed by uncritical political economy continue to be an exemplification of power-centered and totalitarian regimes in Africa.

David Ricardo's Responses to Adam Smith. For Ricardo, exchange value could be objectively measured by the total cost of production. It will be recalled that, for Smith, labor was the ultimate source of value, and money was the measure of that value. Ricardo disagreed with Smith's theory of money as the measure of value since money, like any other commodity, presupposes costs of production, which Ricardo contended Smith did not consider.

---

[40]See the excellent concluding essay of Skinner's Introduction to *The Wealth of Nations* (London: Pelican Classics, 1974), 77-82.

Ricardo suggested that (1) money itself is a commodity which is produced under certain conditions and that until those conditions are analyzed, money cannot serve as an ideal measure of exchange value, and (2) labor is the measure of value as well as the source of value. Ricardo wrote that "the proportion between the quantities of labor necessary for acquiring different objects seems to be the only circumstance which can afford any rule for exchanging them for one another."[41]

Ricardo says further,

> As labor may sometimes purchase a greater, and sometimes a smaller quantity of goods, it is then [the] value [of the goods] which varies, not that of the labor which purchases them; [and therefore] labor, alone never varying in its own value, is alone the ultimate and real standard by which the value of all commodities can at all times and places be estimated and compared.[42]

The debate between Ricardo and Smith revolves around this central insight. To illustrate, consider two commodities such as corn and gold. Imagine that these two commodities are to be exchanged for one another. How is the exchange value of these two commodities to be determined? Following Smith, we can answer the question by stating that the exchange value of these commodities is determined by the amount of labor invested in the production of the commodities. This answer is generally true, Ricardo agrees, but it overlooks a rather fundamental fact; it ignores the role that is played not only by the direct labor that is invested in the production of commodities but also by the indirect "labor that is bestowed on the implements, tools, buildings, with which such [direct] labor is assisted."[43] Even in Smith's rude

---

[41]David Ricardo, *On the Principles of Political Economy and Taxation*, vol. 6 (Cambridge: The University Press for the Royal Economic Society, 1951), 17.

[42]Ricardo, *Principles*, 18.

[43]Ricardo, *Principles*, 22.

society, Ricardo challenges, the hunter necessarily must have used some basic implements, and these implements were produced by labor and cost the hunter some capital. The final labor value must include the labor expended in making the implements and the labor expended in hunting the deer, raising and harvesting the corn, and mining the gold.

The implements and the deer are products of different labor activities which invariably affect the final exchange values of the commodities. In a key passage Ricardo summarized his disputation of Smith:

> If we suppose the occupations of the society extended, that some provide canoes and tackle necessary for fishing, others the seed and rude machinery first used in agriculture, still the same principle would hold true that the exchangeable value of the commodities produced would be in proportion to the labor bestowed on their production; not on their immediate production only, but on all those implements or machines required to give effect to the particular labor to which they were applied.[44]

Throughout this passage, the basic insight that Ricardo added to Smith is that exchange value is not determined alone by labor bestowed directly on commodities but by the total cost of all those modes of labor that indirectly as well as directly contribute to produce the commodities.

Furthermore, argues Ricardo, any improvement of the modes of labor under which a given commodity is produced (such as improvement of the technology of ship construction, which causes a given plant to hire less labor and consequently to lower the cost of production for the capitalist) invariably affects the price of the commodity in that the commodity would exchange for less relative to other commodities. This principle, with minor modification, applies to the exchangeability of all commodities. Therefore, exchange value, says Ricardo, is not solely determined by labor with money as its chief measure, as Smith would have it in modern

---

[44]Ricardo, *Principles*, 24.

society, but also by the total cost of production of all those different commodities which are necessary to produce the commodity being exchanged in the market place.[45] This principle of the total cost or exchange value is modified by "the employment of machinery and other fixed and durable capital."[46] Ricardo said that

> every fall of profit would lower the relative value of these commodities which were produced with a capital of durable nature—machinery for example, and would proportionately elevate those which were produced with capital more perishable. A fall of wages would have precisely the contrary effect.[47]

Also, the more durable the form of capital that a given mode of labor employs, the more the relative value of commodities thusly produced will vary with the fall and rise of wages.[48] In Africa the implications of the rise and fall of wages are quite menacing.

After this groundwork, Ricardo moves toward the quest for a measure of absolute exchange value, a value that is absolute primarily because it would have the capacity to stay above the ever-moving, fluctuating exchange value of commodities which are always affected by the weather, dexterity, ingenuity, industriousness, scarcity or abundance; by the ever-changing nature of the consumer's tastes, habits, customs, psychological dispositions; and by the state of technology and science.[49] If such a commodity could be found, it would have the power to become the ultimate yardstick against which the determination of the exchange value of any commodity could be measured.

---

[45]Ricardo, *Principles*, 24-28.

[46]Ricardo, *Principles*, 35.

[47]Ricardo, *Principles*, 39-40.

[48]Ricardo, *Principles*, 43.

[49]Ricardo, *Principles*, 263.

Such a commodity could not be found. Even gold ultimately is like all other commodities; gold too is subject to those same contingencies under which all commodities are produced. As Ricardo puts it, and this is his central insight,

> Neither gold then nor any other commodity can ever be a perfect measure of value for all things; but I have already remarked that the effect on the relative price of things, from a variation of profits, is comparatively slight; that by far the most important effects are produced by the varying quantities of labor required for production; and therefore, if we suppose this important cause of variation removed from the production of gold, we shall probably possess as near an approximation to a standard measure as can be theoretically conceived.[50]

In other words, Ricardo concludes his analysis of value with the claim that he stands alone against the tradition of Smith and others with his original insight that a rise in the price of labor would *not* be followed by a rise in the price of commodities, primarily because commodities are produced with the aid of durable and nondurable capital and that only the price of those commodities that employ more durable capital "would positively fall in price when wages rose." In his own words,

> I have not said, because one commodity has so much labor bestowed upon it or will cost 1000£ and another so much or will cost 1000£ that therefore one would be of the value of 1000£ and the other of the value of 2000£, but I have said that their value will be to each other on two to one, and that in those proportions they will be exchangéd. I affirm only that their relative values will be governed by the relative qualities of labor bestowed on their production.[51]

---

[50]Ricardo, *Principles*, 45.

[51]Ricardo, *Principles*, 47.

Finally, Ricardo was aware of Smith's three-class theory of a harmonious economic whole. Ricardo also was silent about the implications of the domination of the owning group of people over the working people; rather, as an economist, he is interested in the analysis of the determination of price in an economic whole composed of classes, and the distribution of commodities among and between the capitalists, landlords, and laborers. The relationship of the three classes, he argues, economically speaking implies a relationship among the three economic categories: profit, rent, and wages.[52] The rise or fall of rent, profit, and wages is directly conditioned by the power relationships among the human beings who stand behind the economic categories.

Ricardo also was equally aware of the implications of the extension of the market system across borders and the incentive to accumulate capital with an eye on the comparative advantage to the economically disadvantaged.[53] Ricardo's ideal economic distribution was that in which all the nations of the world under a free trade system would import goods from those nations that could produce the goods more cheaply and efficiently than they could be produced at home, and would export other goods that are profitable to export and money-saving to produce at home. If all nations could excel in the production, distribution, and exportation of those natural resources which they possess, and participate in a world economy, humankind would lead a better life. However, experience teaches that human beings, because of mistrust of each other, prefer to "be satisfied with a low rate of profit in their own country, rather than seek a more advantageous employment for their wealth in foreign nations."[54] If one could establish an authentic free trade system, one free of classes, Africa could play a major role in the world trade system based upon the development of its mineral resources.

The minimal condition for a better life, as Ricardo observed, is the need for human beings to trust one another. It is rational and intelligent to develop a community founded upon trust as

---

[52]Ricardo, *Principles*, 49.

[53]Ricardo, *Principles*, 132.

[54]Ricardo, *Principles*, 137.

opposed to mistrust, cooperation as opposed to competition, and well-coordinated and honest production, distribution, and consumption of world resources. Africa's material resources, as well as the humane endowments of some of its inhabitants, could play a major role in the construction of an ethical community. Such an ethical community would have to be inhabited by healthy souls, but these are lacking in the world today. African resources, however, are systematically exploited in a manner reminiscent of the ideas of Karl Marx, to whose ideas we now turn.

3

CONFLICTS IN POLITICAL ECONOMY

Marx's Analysis of Exploitation

Karl Marx, a classical German critical philosopher, provides a masterful critique of classical political economy and especially of Adam Smith and David Ricardo. For Marx, there is no objective measure of value; labor is grounded upon a systematic theory of exploitation at the point of production. Marx's major premise, in which he implicitly disagrees with Smith and Ricardo's, is as follows:

> Wages are determined by the fierce struggle between capitalist and worker. The capitalist inevitably wins. The capitalist can live longer without the worker than the worker can live without him. Combination among capitalists is habitual and effective, while combination among the workers is forbidden and has painful consequences for them.[1]

In the determination of value via the determination of wages, the normal wage according to Adam Smith, Marx contends, is the amount of money which enables a person to live a bestial existence.[2] The wages that the worker gets is disproportional to the amount of labor that the worker has invested in the production of the commodity, hence the determination of wages is based upon exploitation.

---

[1]Karl Marx, *Early Writing* (New York: Vintage Books, 1975), 282.

[2]Marx, *Early Writing*, 282.

Every gain for the capitalist is followed not by a similar gain for the worker but by a loss for the worker. Sometimes when the market prices of commodities are lowered, the capitalist loses some profit, but the worker loses part of his or her subsistence. When the wealth of society decreases, the worker suffers most; when the wealth of society increases, the worker is expected to overwork and sacrifice his or her freedom and become a slave of work. Overwork leads to increase in the division of labor which further leads to overspecialization and the end of intimate, nonalienated work.

Marx noted that

a society of which the greater part suffers is not happy. But since even the most prosperous state of society leads to suffering for the majority and since the economic system, Nationalokonomie, which is a society based on private interest, brings about such a state of prosperity, it follows that society's distress is the goal of the economic system.[3]

Marx tells us that for political economy in theory the whole produce of labor belongs to the worker, but the worker gets only a portion of that produce, the absolute minimum; that the worker is the lord of nature as an active laboring being; that labor is a constant measure of value but in reality nothing is further from the truth in that the price of commodities is forever fluctuating; that the division of labor leads to the refinement of society and at the same time impoverishes the workers by rendering their labor, their produce, and their relationship with nature alien to themselves.[4] Capital praises the workers when they are actively engaged in productive labor, but capital despises the workers when they cannot work and beget capital. In essence, Marx concludes from his empirical observations of the conditions of the worker and his theoretical dialectical analysis that political economy contradicts itself. It is simply engaging itself in "double think."

---

[3]Marx, *Early Writing*, 286.

[4]Marx, *Early Writing*, 286.

For Marx, political economists are guilty of considering humankind only as an economically indispensable source of abstract labor, and that abstract labor is a wage-earning activity. Marx puts it lucidly, "political economy regards labor abstractly as a thing; labor is a commodity; if the price [of a given commodity] is high, the commodity is much in demand; if it is low then it is much in supply; the price of labor as a commodity must fall lower and lower."[5] This price differentiation is brought about partly by the competition among the workers themselves. The wage is a commodity of unfortunate characteristics in that misery, unhappiness, and squalid working conditions are what it obtains for the worker. Marx wrote as follows:

> Ricardo in his book (*On the Principles of Political Economy and Taxation*) says Nations are merely work-shops for production, and man is a machine for consuming and producing. Human life is a piece of capital. Economic laws rule the world blindly. For Ricardo, men are nothing, the product everything.[6]

Marx explores the relationships among classes to which Smith and Ricardo allude. Marx then proceeds to ask the same question that Smith and Ricardo asked, but which they never fully answered: What is the basis of capital, that is, of private property? The basis of capital is the existence of a capitalist, who by the legally sanctified positive law acquires the right to own productive stock, which in turn enables him to own a seemingly purely economic power: the power to purchase. With the purchasing power, the capitalist also acquires political power. Purchasing power is simultaneously political economic power. Purchasing political economic power is "therefore the power to command labor and its products. The capitalist possesses this power not on account of his or her personal or human properties but insofar as he or she is an owner of capital. His power is the purchasing

---

[5]Marx, *Early Writing*, 246-88; See also Marx's famous discussion of estranged labor on pp. 322-58 as a further development of his discussions here.

[6]Marx, *Early Writing*, 306.

power of capital, which nothing can withstand."[7] Above it is the capitalist that seems to have a complete domination over capital and thus the laboring process as a whole. However, capital itself is sometimes "able to rule the capitalist himself."[8] But then, what is capital?

Capital is stored-up labor, labor that is stocked and then stored up. Stock is only called capital when it provides its owner with a revenue or profit. Here Marx closely follows Smith's argument in order to refute it by pointing out internal contradictions. The capitalist employs the laborer not out of any humanistic purposes but because the laborer, when properly managed, can and does serve as the source of profit. In a bold passage, Marx quotes Smith:

> The consideration of his own private profit is the sole motive which determines the owner of any capital to employ it either in agriculture, in manufactures, or in some particular branch of the wholesale or retail trade. The different quantities of productive labor which it may put into motion, and the different values which it may add to the annual produce of the land and labor of the society, according as it is employed in one or other of those different ways, never enter into his thoughts.[9]

Of course, Marx adds, wages are raised and lowered, profits are increased and decreased as a result of competition among capitalists, just as the rent of land is raised and lowered as a result of competition among landlords who are or become capitalists.[10] The logic of the relationship among industrialists is the same as that among landlords. Throughout political economy, the various struggles between capitalists/workers, landlords/tenants, particular

---

[7]Marx, *Early Writing*, 295.

[8]Marx, *Early Writing*, 295.

[9]Marx, *Early Writing*, 298-99.

[10]Marx, *Early Writing*, 299.

interests/universal interests, Marx says, are perpetuated and perpetuated through the ideology and power of social organization.[11]

Marx challenges one of the central themes in classical political economy, namely, the question of the determination of value. It will be recalled that for Smith labor as a measurement of value never changes. Marx quotes Smith as follows:

> A definite amount of labor is always a definite amount of labor for the worker—whether I obtain much or little for an hour of work—which depends on its productivity and other circumstances. I have worked one hour. What I have had to pay for the result of my work, my wages, is always the same hour of work. . . .[12]

Marx disagrees with this central proposition. Marx's disagreement, as will be indicated soon, is reminiscent of Ricardo's reservations about the problem of establishing absolute value.

Marx agrees with Smith that labor is the source of all value. Labor for Smith, however, is neither a joyous nor a liberating activity; it is simply a necessary means with which we exist on earth. In fact, says Smith, labor is a curse. Marx fundamentally disagrees with the idea of labor as a curse. For Marx, labor is a mode of transforming external nature.

Marx is right that labor is a mode of transforming external nature, but it is misleading for Marx to assert that external nature should be transformed in spite of the conditions under which the transformation takes place. Marx's statement needs some explicit limiting conditions which I wish to provide. The prescientific

---

[11]Marx, *Early Writing*, 299.

[12]Marx, *Early Writing*, 306. The quotation from Ricardo is from his French translation, chapter 26. It reads, "To an individual with a capital of £20,000, whose profits were 2,000 per annum, it would be a matter quite indifferent whether his capital would employ a hundred or a thousand men. . . is not the real interest of the nation similar? Provided its net real income, its rents and profits be the same, it is of no importance whether the nation consists of ten or twelve million inhabitants? (p. 300)."

African view of external nature is one such limiting condition that Marx's general statement requires. The prescientific African view would not transform external nature merely because it is technically possible. Rather, such a view would be guided by such reasonable and moral views of external nature which state that it is intrinsically worthy of our respect because it is a complete end in itself; its various parts—stones, animals, minerals, and plants—also have a silent dignity of their own that humans cannot thoughtlessly violate; the parts of external nature that we absolutely need for our humanity must be carefully and reflectively transformed; and the transformation of external nature must at all times be done by the intelligent and gentle guidance of a morally-sensitive technology.

It is during humankind's transformation of external nature that we see the disclosure of human power, the power to make and unmake nature according to basic human rules which are regulated by thought, imagination, and compassion. The laboring activity when broadly conceived makes it possible for humankind to exercise thoughtfully its intelligence and moral power. Labor is to human activity as thought is to the human mind in that labor allows us to disclose our true selves just as logical categories enable us to understand an otherwise complex world. In this extended sense, humankind does not engage in labor because it is cursed to do so, as a version of the biblical tradition argues. Rather, humankind is endowed with the basic faculties of thought, intelligence, imagination, language, and moral power through which it emancipates itself from the constraining conditions of nature. The objective of transforming nature is not to master it blindly by doing violence to it. Rather, the goal is to treat nature as an ethical and aesthetical companion of humankind which is to be given human shape in such a way that it serves human purposes and needs. When Marx says that labor is not a curse but rather a liberating activity, he has the above strong interpretation of labor in mind.

Although Marx agrees with Smith that wage labor is a curse, it does not follow that labor indeed is a curse. Of course, Smith is right in one sense: the various forms of slave and wage labor in no way could be regarded as liberating. As defined by Marx these are forced labors. Real labor on the other hand inherently conceives the above forms of labor as embodiments of unfreedom

94

and unhappiness. Labor carries this double meaning: a potential road toward freedom and happiness and an actual reality of unfreedom and unhappiness. The wage labor of Smith is an activity which spiritually impoverishes rather than enriching people. Real labor, which Marx sometimes calls free working, however, cannot and is not intended to mean play as Fourier thinks.[13] Marx says in fact:

> Really free working, e.g., composing, is at the same time the most damned seriousness, the most intense exertion. The work of material production can achieve this character only (1) when its social character is posited, (2) when it is of a scientific and at the same time general character, not merely human exertion as a specifically harnessed natural force, but exertion as subject, which appears in the production process not in a merely natural, spontaneous form, but as an activity regulating all the forces of nature. Adam Smith, by the way, has only the slaves of capital in mind.[14]

Marx suggests that an alternative form of labor can be developed, one which is nonalienated labor and freed from domination and which respects the intrinsic dignity of human beings. Thus to regard wage labor as if it is the only kind of labor that the human engages in is a mistake. Smith's conception of labor, says Marx, naturalizes and thus dogmatizes a historically specific form of labor (wage labor) to which humans through education, custom, and habit became systematically socialized. Furthermore for Smith labor time or the amount of labor is the measure of values; thus commodity A which took two hours to produce would be sold at a price commensurate with two hours' work, at say $10 per hour would be $20 for two hours. Its value is thus $20.00. But to say that labor time is the measure of value "means nothing other than that the measure of labor is the

[13]Karl Marx, *Grundrisse* (New York: Vintage Books, 1975), 611.

[14]Marx, *Grundrisse*, 611.

measure of values."[15]   True, says Marx, the measure of labor is time.   There are different forms of labor activity, however, each form requiring different investments of time and different skills such that philosophizing is different from composing.   Of course, in a very general sense these two forms of labor are similar in that they both require cerebral and muscular exertion.   Each activity embodies different lengths of time.   Neither of these two forms of labor produces capital in Smith's strict conception of labor as producing capital.   They make the point, however, that both are forms of labor in a general sense and that time operates in these activities as a measure of their value independent of their not producing capital.   They are examples of Marx's loose, less economical but more philosophical interpretation of labor as a specific form of human activity that creates a human world, and in which economic activity is merely one aspect of a larger concept of activity.   In a passage that directly contradicts Smith's political economy but neglects his profound moral theory, Marx writes,

> Only because products are labor, can they be measured
> by the measure of labor, by labor time, the amount of
> labor consumed in them. The negation of tranquility,
> as mere negation, ascetic sacrifice, creates nothing.
> Someone may castigate and flagellate himself all day
> long like the monks etc., and this quantity of sacrifice
> he contributes will remain totally worthless.   The
> natural price of things is not the sacrifice made for
> them.[16]

For Marx, labor as a positive, creative activity that produces material objects as a result of its purposeful transformation of nature is of course measured by time.   But time itself does not depend on the productivity of labor to gain its worth; labor's productivity is always the same everywhere.   "The values of products are measured not by the labor employed in them, but by labor necessary for their production. Hence not sacrifice, but labor

---

[15]Marx, *Grundrisse*, 612.

[16]Marx, *Grundrisse*, 613.

is a condition of production."[17] Similarly, Marx proceeds attack Smith's derivation of the necessity of profit by saying that in the rude society, the derivation of profit was unnecessary in that the product of labor wholly belonged to the producer. In the industrial society that Smith examines, the interconnected economic whole seemingly divided labor and the products of labor as fairly as possible among the capitalists, landlords, and laborers. The capitalist in particular expects to derive maximal profit for his contribution, and the capitalists and their profits are part of capital. This particular derivation of profit is once again attacked by Marx as naive. Smith, according to Marx, does not understand the complex interconnections of capital. Capital is a form of social relation that hides a series of human conflicts. Behind the apparent harmony of Smith's ideal lies a potentially explosive conflict of human interests, wishes, and aspirations. In his investigation of Smith's political economy which he often admires Marx uncovers a system of exploitation: exploitation of human by human that Smith's theory hides.

Marx says that Ricardo's theory of value is more advanced than Smith's, but Ricardo did not have a theory of exploitation. According to Marx, it is chiefly Ricardo who understood that capital rules labor or that capital perpetuates itself not merely by creating exchange value through producing commodities which are destined for the market under wage labor, but capital governs subtly by the extraction of surplus value. Such value is a necessary and sufficient condition for the production of profit and hence the enrichment of the capitalist and the poverty of the laborer because surplus value is extracted directly at the point of production from the "toil and trouble" of labor.

Ricardo alone understood the process of extracting surplus value through his relentless efforts to understand the deep phenomenon of the underworld of Smith's deer hunter's implements, the conditions of the coming into being of the implements themselves, their cost of production, the natural environment in which the tools find themselves, and the wages of the toilers. Of course, Ricardo drew necessary attention to all of the above details of production, but he did not go as far as Marx in developing a

---

[17]Marx, *Grundrisse*, 614.

theory of labor exploitation at the point of production. For Ricardo, as was noted earlier, the question was not an analysis of how A exploits B, but rather how does A pay B, how does A determine (1) the value of the commodities that B produces, and (2) the wage that B receives as a consequence of (1). Ricardo, who essentially builds upon Smith's conception of the economic whole, conceives of the human relations of wage labor as natural, given a necessary human order. In his analysis of international trade, for example, Ricardo thinks more about wealth, and how the accumulation of wealth if properly distributed would lead to international tranquility. Again, in divorcing wealth from value, Ricardo falls into the error of separating the relationship between distribution and production, which for Marx is a methodological sin. For Marx, labor as such is a totality of production, distribution, exchange, and consumption. To examine any of these steps in isolation leaves the analysis of labor incomplete, a partial grasp of the whole. An analysis of value or wealth must be based on the grasp of the life of the entire production, distribution, exchange, and consumption process. Ricardo analyzes the economic whole frequently by concentrating on a single step to the exclusion of the other steps. His separation of value and wealth is a classic example of the tendency.[18] The antithesis which Ricardo created between wealth and value is a false one in that wealth cannot be understood without value and value cannot be illustrated without wealth; each illuminates the other.[19]

What is Ricardo's theory of value as Marx understands it? For Ricardo, Marx says, the production costs of goods determine their exchange value, and in this form it appears that exchange value is the only form of value. For Ricardo, the Marxian concept of use value does not exist; all value is exchange value. Furthermore, there is no distinction between surplus value and profit for Ricardo, but such a distinction is the necessary condition for a given capitalist, who by extracting a surplus of labor and a surplus of time from a given laborer manages to secure values for which

---

[18]Marx, *Grundrisse*, 615.

[19]Marx, *Grundrisse*, 615. See Marx's seminal discussion of method, which is heavily influenced by Hegel's *Logic*, in his introduction to the *Grundrisse*, pp. 81-113.

the laborer is unpaid. During the act of production itself, and not during the period of distribution on which Ricardo focuses, the capitalist already obtains from the laborer the capital he needs, a condition necessary for the accumulation of profit. It is at the point of production and not at the point of distribution, Marx contends, that systematic exploitation of humans by humans begins. Of course, the process does not end there; the process extends itself to become a feature of all the remaining steps in the process of labor as a totality: distribution, exchange, and consumption. The real problem of Ricardo's economics, says Marx, is that Ricardo never asks the question, How is value created. Rather he asks, How is it distributed. The question Ricardo asks inevitably led him to concentrate not on production but on distribution, not on totality but on particularity, not on the whole but on the part. In a key passage, Marx writes,

> Besides, this [human] clashes with sound common sense because the capitalist knows very well that he counts wages and profit among the production costs and regulates the necessary price accordingly. This contradiction in the determination of the product by relative labor time, and the limitation of the sum of profit and wages by the sum of this labor time, and the real determination of prices in practice, comes about only because profit is not grasped as itself a derivative, secondary form of surplus value, the same is true of what the capitalist justly regards, [that is, the profit factor which he builds into production costs], as his production costs. His profit arises simply from the fact that a part of the cost of production costs him nothing, hence does not enter into his "outlays," his production costs.[20]

Marx's crucial complaints in his confrontations of both Smith and Ricardo are that (1) both are unconscious of the fact that capital is founded upon the extraction of surplus value, an ingenious method of exploitation of the laborer by the capitalist;

---

[20]Marx, *Grundrisse*, 554.

(2) exploitation itself, which is morally reprehensible, was not of direct concern to either of them; and (3) the exploitation of humans by humans is morally wrong because his theory of exploitation is based on his analysis of surplus value and was stimulated by a moral judgment which he does not explicitly avow. Marx makes it incumbent upon himself to show a "scientific" demonstration of the existence of exploitation in capitalist economy since neither Smith in his *The Theory of Moral Sentiments* nor Ricardo seemed to be exclusively concerned about the moral dimension of political economy.

Marx's Theory of Exploitation and Surplus Value

Because Smith was intensely sensitive to the moral phenomena of exploitation in his moral theory, Smith's readers, of which Marx was one, cannot neglect his moral dimension and judge him solely by his economic work. Although Smith might have known nothing about Marx's theory of surplus value, he was morally sensitive to its possibility. But for Ricardo perhaps the exercise of moral thinking was unimportant. It is fair then to say of Marx that it was he who with his theory of surplus value directly and systematically exposed classical political economy as deeply affected by an exploitative form of immorality. Such immorality justified itself for the sake of a new capitalist political economy which could give moral value to capital accumulation for a small number of people and ignore the rest of humanity. The food crisis in Africa is an example of exploitation at the point of production. What are the chief elements of Marx's theory of surplus value? For Marx, the meaning of value influences the meaning of surplus value. The first category in which "bourgeois wealth" presents itself is the category of commodity. For Marx, the commodity has two values: use value, its capacity to satisfy human need, for example, the wheat from which bread is made; and exchange value, its capacity to be sold at a market for a definite price. Exchange value is the more dominant form of value in capitalistic economies. Under capital, use values take on the appearance of exchange values and then eventually become exchange values. Marx's preoccupation in his economic works was to expose the inner architectonic of exploitation that is hidden from most people. Marx's surplus value focuses on the significant moment in which use value is transformed into exchange value. Thus, says Marx,

> Wheat, e.g., possesses the same use value, whether cultivated by slaves, serfs or free laborers. It would not lose its use value if it fell from the sky like snow. Now how does use value become transformed into a commodity, a vehicle of exchange value?[21]

It is Marx's thesis that the capitalist does not invest capital in the production of commodities for the sake of their capacity to fulfill human needs; that is, for the sake of the use values of commodities.[22] The capitalist invests in commodities for the sake of their capacity to be exchanged for money; that is, for their exchange value which produces more capital. Therefore, use values are important to the capitalist only insofar as they are depositories of exchange value. In a passage that sums up his conception of surplus value, Marx writes,

> Our capitalist has two objects in view: in the first place, he wants to produce a use value that has a value in exchange, that is to say, an article destined to be sold, a commodity; and secondly, he desires to produce a commodity whose value shall be greater than the sum of the values of the commodities used in its production, that is of the means of production and the labor power that he purchased with good money in the open market. His aim is to produce not only a use value, but a commodity also, not only use value, but value; not only value, but at the same time surplus value.[23]

---

[21]Marx, *Grundrisse*, 881.

[22]Marx, *Grundrisse*, 881. Also see Marx, *Capital* (New York: International Publishers), 186.

[23]Marx, *Capital*, 186.

In the above passage, Marx attacks Smith's thesis that value is determined by labor as such (full compensation for the laborer's toil and trouble) and also disagrees with Ricardo's claim that value is determined not merely by the laborer's toil and trouble but by the total cost of production. For Ricardo, the toil and trouble are fully remunerated as wages, and the wages are the explicit determinations of the values that the laborer creates. Marx disagrees with Ricardo by stating that both the toil and trouble as well as the remuneration of the costs of production do not include the surplus values that the laborer creates and for which he or she is never fully paid. The laborer creates values, surplus values, and these values are then reproduced in a form that is alien to the laborer. The surplus values that are the genuine products of the laborer's intimate work on external nature (cotton, wood, steel, rubber) are converted into commodities destined to be exchanged for money from which the capitalist makes profit.

The commodities that the African peasantry produces are inherently based upon the extraction of surplus value at the point of production for which the peasant producer of commodities is never paid or compensated. The Nigerian producer of cocoa, the Ethiopian producer of coffee, the Sudanese producer of cotton, the South African producer of gold, and the Liberian producer of rubber are creating surplus values at the point of production for which they are never fully compensated. To the extent (1) that Africans are producing commodities destined to be exchanged for money, (2) that they produce commodities which become alien to them and belong to capitalists, (3) that capitalists make profits at the African's expense, it follows (4) that the material suffering of Africans is grounded upon a specific theory of the exploitation of man by man at the point of production through the systematic extraction of surplus value.

According to the general law of value, which Marx illustrates, surplus value is produced in the following way:

> Let us examine the matter more closely. The value of a day's labor-power amounts to 3 shillings, because on our assumption half a day's labor is embodied in that quantity of labor-power, i.e., because the means of subsistence that are daily required for the production of labor-power, cost half a day's labor. But the past

labor that is embodied in the labor-power, and the living labor that it can call into action; the daily cost of maintaining it, and its daily expenditure in work, are two totally different things. The former determines the exchange-value of the labor-power, the latter is its use-value. The fact that half a day's labor is necessary to keep the laborer alive during 24 hours does not in any way prevent him from working a whole day. Therefore, the value of labor-power, and the value which that labor-power creates in the labor-process are two entirely different magnitudes; and this difference of the two values was what the capitalist had in view when he was purchasing the labor-power. The useful qualities that labor-power possesses, and by virtue of which it makes yarn or boots, were to him nothing more than a *conditio sine qua non*; for in order to create value, labor must be expended in a useful manner. What really influenced him was the specific use-value which this commodity possesses of being a source not only of value, but of more value than it has itself. This is the special service that the capitalist expects from labor-power, and in this transaction he acts in accordance with the "eternal laws" of the exchange of commodities. The seller of labor-power, like the seller of any other commodity, realizes its exchange-value and parts with its use-value. He cannot take the one without giving the other. The use-value of labor-power, or in other words, labor, belongs just as little to its seller, as the use-value of oil after it has been sold belongs to the dealer who has sold it. The owner of the money has paid the value of a day's labor-power, his, therefore, is the use of it for a day, a day's labor belongs to him. The circumstance, that on the one hand the daily sustenance of labor-power costs only half a day's labor, while on the other hand the very same labor-power can work during a whole day, that consequently the value which its use during one day creates, is double what he pays for that use, this circumstance is, without doubt, a piece of good luck for the buyer, but by no means an injury to the seller.

Our capitalist foresaw this state of things, and that was the cause of his laughter. The laborer therefore finds, in the workshop, the means of production necessary for working, not only during six, but during twelve hours. Just as during the six hours' process our 10 lbs. of cotton absorbed six hours' labor, and became 10 lbs. of yarn, so now 20 lbs. of cotton will absorb 12 hours' labor and be changed into 20 lbs. of yarn. Let us now examine the product of this prolonged process. There is now materialized in this 20 lbs. of yarn the labor of five days, of which four days are due to the cotton and the lost steel of the spindle, the remaining day having been absorbed by the cotton during the spinning process. Expressed in gold, the labor of five days is thirty shillings. This is therefore the price of the 20 lbs. of yarn, giving, as before, eighteen pence as the price of a pound. But the sum of the values of the commodities that entered into the process amounts to 27 shillings. The value of the yarn is 30 shillings. Therefore the value of the product is 1/9 greater than the value advanced for its production; 27 shillings have been transformed into 30 shillings; a surplus-value of 3 shillings has been created. The trick has at last succeeded; money has been converted into capital.[24]

But the process described as a trick by Marx must have a validity from the perspective of the capitalist. The validity is based on the following hypothetical argument. Put the following question to the capitalist: how do you think you deserve the creation of the three shillings surplus value? He or she might say, "I provided the laborer with all the necessary material equipment that he or she needed to produce the yarn. It was I who for instance provided the machinery, the plant, the cotton, and the spindle. The laborer sold his or her labor to me. I rendered an indispensable service by my instrument of production to the whole of society. I therefore deserve to be given a return for my services. True, my laborer has returned to me the service I gave to society

---

[24]Marx, *Capital*, 194.

with an equivalent service in that my cotton and spindle have become yarn by toil and trouble. But I have worked as well in the production of the yarn: I superintended and overlooked the laboring process"—although in reality it is his managers who did the above as well. But the capitalist is not ashamed to give credit to himself or herself when credit is not due, nor does he or she in the final analysis care to reason from premises to valid conclusions. The capitalist is a practical business person. He or she does not care to give a nonnaturalistic explanation of the genesis of the exploitation of man by man. He or she simply exploits. In short, it is the exploitation of humans by humans which Marx's morally inclined political economy attempted to describe. We now turn to an examination of the extent to which Marx's theory is applicable to modern Africa.

Africa's Resources and Amoral Political Economy

For a long time the exploitation of humans by humans has existed in Africa. There, the toil and trouble of the labor of Africans continues to be subject to exploitation along the lines that Marx has described. The lingering presence in Africa of famine, hunger, political injustice, and human unhappiness—the classical foci of moral philosophy—continues to compel close attention.

I have attempted to explain the African food crisis in chapter 1 and the larger phenomenon of the predicament of African underdevelopment in chapter 2. My concern now is to contribute toward the alleviation of hunger and political injustice. My goal is to synthesize morality and political economy, to provide a foundation of how discourses in moral philosophy combined with the tasks of political economy may enable us to examine systematically the themes of famine, hunger, unhappiness, and political injustice.

It is the thesis of this book that the human condition in Africa is an example of material underdevelopment and a classic focus to which theories of political economy may be applied. This material underdevelopment could be overcome if humankind's moral powers were attentive to those who are hungry, unhappy, and politically enslaved by the political economic power of capital as a natural state of being, whose presence in Africa rarely is questioned from the standpoint of what is morally just. To engage in such questioning is to think directly about exploitation of humans by humans. In this sense Marx's morally inclined theory of exploitation still is relevant to any discussion of the human condition in Africa. Marx's theory of exploitation and alienation must be combined with an explicit moral theory, such as the sections on the moral functions of the social passions in Smith's *Theory of Moral Sentiments*. I intend to use Smith's moral theory in my attempt at constructing a theory which combines morality and political economy in overcoming material underdevelopment in Africa.

In talking about Smith, I combined his profound moral visions of a good community with his strict political economy of a capitalist economic whole. There lies a tension in Smith as a moral thinker because of his moral vision which is conscious of the possibility of the exploitation of humans, his attempts to regulate exploitation by the moral ideals of sympathy, and his vision of the economic whole that makes certain forms of exploitation necessary. Had Smith written a book synthesizing his moral theory and political economy, what would he have emphasized? Would he have emphasized the role of the unsocial passions plus the selfish ones and constructed a capitalist society that condones exploitation as natural, or would he have emphasized the role of the social passions and constructed a moral community based on the ideals of social cooperation without classes? These are very difficult questions. Marx severely criticized Smith's political economy but was silent about his moral theory. Had Marx studied *The Theory of Moral Sentiments*, he might have found that the moral theory which produced the political economy was wanting. Marx might have rejected it simply as "bourgeois." Had Marx studied Smith's moral theory, particularly its analysis of the social passions, he might have used them as pillars upon which could stand his own vision of the community of nonalienated laborers. Marx missed an opportunity to construct an alternative relationship of political economy and morality which requires no exploitation of human beings by human beings. I intend to use the idea of the social passions and present a theory of political economy and morality that applies to the African human condition characterized by material poverty, unfreedom, and unhappiness.

Smith's Conceptions of Economics and Morality

The reasons behind our interest in Smith's moral theory are two. The first is that economics is not an exact science, free of moral value. The fact that Adam Smith began his career as a thinker by working on a book of moral theory indicates his conviction either that economic theories are premised by moral assumptions or that economic categories conceal moral categories. The second reason is that we may infer that Smith's classical economic theory was in fact profoundly moral in its vision of humankind's capacity to live a good and happy life. The question then is not whether classical political economy as advanced by Smith is or is not a moral theory, but rather what kinds of moral theories did Smith advance. In what particular ways did his moral theory influence or determine his analysis of the economic whole summarized above?

The opening paragraph of *The Theory of Moral Sentiments* reads,

> How selfish so ever man may be supposed, there are evidently some principles in his nature, which interest him in the fortune of others, and render their happiness necessary to him, though he derives nothing from it except the pleasure of seeing it. Of this kind is pity or compassion, the emotion which we feel for the misery of others, when we either see it or are made to conceive it in a very lively manner. That we often derive sorrow from the sorrow of others is a matter of fact too obvious to require any instances to prove it; for the sentiment, like all the other original passions of human nature, is by no means confined to the virtuous and humane, though they perhaps may feel it with the most exquisite sensibility. The greatest ruffian, the most hardened violator of the laws of society is not altogether without it.[25]

---

[25]Adam Smith, *The Theory of Moral Sentiments* (Oxford: Clarendon Press, 1976), 8.

In the above passage, Smith advances a theory of humankind's moral composition that was one of the boldest of his day. He was influenced perhaps by David Hume, an equally strongly determined moral philosopher. For Smith, the human person is a passionate moral being; some of his or her passions are unsocial (anger, resentment, hate), but other passions are social (generosity, humanity, kindness, compassion, mutual friendship and esteem). When the social passions are exercised with a measure of delicacy and balance, they are exceptionally useful for the solidification of human relations.

Moreover, there are what Smith calls selfish passions. These passions constitute the middle place between the social and unsocial passions. Grief and joy are examples. These selfish passions were of paramount importance in Smith's *The Wealth of Nations*.

For Smith, human beings are definitely endowed with moral sentiments. When men and women, as owners of capital and thus investors in a profitable business, employ other people to work for them, they sometimes love and sometimes hate those other people. Social interaction with their employees has a distinct economic nature. Interactions among people have an economic form governed by a specific moral premise arising from the unsocial and selfish passions. At this point, Smith's moral theory directly influences his political economic model of the good society. In its economic dealings, we can infer from the above quotation, humankind has a divided concept of the self. Thus in *The Wealth of Nations*,

> It is not from the benevolence of the butcher, the brewer, or the baker that we expect our dinner, but from their regard to their own interest. We address ourselves, not to their humanity but to their self-love, and never talk to them of our own necessities but of their advantages. Nobody but a beggar chooses to depend chiefly upon the benevolence of his fellow-citizens.[26]

---

[26]Smith, *Wealth*, 119.

The thesis of *The Theory of Moral Sentiment* is that the human self, when it engages its moral (social) power, is exceptionally sympathetic and is cautiously selfish and self-regarding in its economic life. Compared with the quotation, it seems from *The Wealth of Nations* that Smith is contradictory. In fact, he is not since in his moral theory he has equipped us already with the argument that people have social, unsocial, and selfish passions in everyday life.

The essence of a human being's moral life is sympathy, contends Smith. "The word sympathy, in its most proper and primitive significance, denotes our fellow-feeling with the sufferings, not that with the enjoyments of others."[27] This strong interpretation of sympathy is crucial for the understanding of Smith's moral theory. Smith adds, "our sympathy with sorrow is, in some sense, more universal than that with joy. Though sorrow is excessive, we may still have some fellow-feeling with it."[28] Furthermore, the sufferers will strongly deserve our sympathy if they silently undergo their pain and sorrow with a self-esteem that compels our admiration and moral action.

There are various kinds of sympathies. One aspect of human passions tends to draw our sympathy away from the condition of those in sorrow or deprivation, and direct it toward those who are happy, powerful, or rich. This disposition to admire the rich and look down upon the poor, Smith contends, is not the refinement and growth of our moral sentiments; rather it is the corruption of moral sentiments. The latter disposition was so much part of humanity's moral life throughout all ages that its pervasive existence continues to command the attention of moral philosophers. Smith himself in his *The Moral Sentiments* does not address the problem of cleansing an individual's corruption, but in his political economy in the sections on justice he leaves it as a task for the state when moral sentiments become so corrupt that they prevent the harmonious working of the economy. We may infer from Smith's moral theory that if the luxury, happiness, and comfort of some human beings results in the poverty, pain, and inconvenience of others, if an individual's social and moral sentiments of

---

[27]Smith, *Moral Sentiments*, 43.

[28]Smith, *Moral Sentiments*, 43-44.

sympathy are corrupted or a person is indifferent to those who are suffering, the society as a whole will be not only morally corrupt but also economically inefficient. Smith says the following in his *The Wealth of Nations*:

> Servants, laborers, and workmen of different kind, make up the far greater part of every great political society. But what improves the circumstances of the greater part can never be regarded as an inconveniency to the whole. No society can surely be flourishing and happy, of which the far greater parts of the members are poor and miserable. It is but equity, besides, that they who feed, clothe, and lodge the whole body of the people, should have such a share of the produce of their own labor as to be themselves tolerably well fed, clothed, and lodged.[29]

Clearly, the above paragraph is premised on the moral arguments of *The Theory of Moral Sentiments*. Perhaps the most important of Smith's moral arguments for African economy theorists is his examination of justice and the consequences of injustice. He comments on the perpetuation of acts of injustice as follows:

> The violator of the more sacred laws of justice can never reflect on the sentiments which mankind must entertain with regard to him, without feeling all the agonies of shame, and horror, and consternation. When his passion is gratified, and he begins coolly to reflect on his past conduct, he can enter into none of the motives which influenced it. They appear now as detestable to him as they did always to other people. By sympathizing with the hatred and abhorrence which other men must entertain for him, he becomes in some measure the object of his own hatred and abhorrence. The situation of the person, who suffered by his injustice, now calls upon his pity. He is grieved at the

---

[29]Smith, *Wealth*, 181.

110

thought of it; regrets the unhappy effects of his own conduct, and feels at the same time that they have rendered him the proper object of the resentment and indignation of mankind, and of what is the natural consequence of resentment, vengeance, and punishment.[30]

For Smith, no society can subsist where injustices are tolerated, and no human intercourse, even economic, can prevail without a measure of love, self-love, self-respect, self-command, economic equality, and a sense of duty combined with a respect of the moral law embodied in the respect of the deity.[31]

Our moral sentiments, Smith contends, are influenced by custom in that what is customary is seldom questioned but uncritically absorbed; but custom affects our moral integrity. Often by blindly following customs, we live the unexamined life, the thoughtless and conscienceless life. A genuine moral theory should subject custom to a severe examination on the behalf of the moral sentiments.[32] In a characteristic passage, Smith argues that

when custom can give sanction to so dreadful a violation of humanity, we may well imagine that there is scarcely any particular practice so gross which it cannot authorize. Such a thing, we hear men everyday saying, is commonly done, and they seem to think this is a sufficient apology for what, in itself, is the most unjust and unreasonable conduct.[33]

Smith's assertions can be considered to mean that political society (government) and civil society are composed of individuals. The totality of these unique but in certain respects similar individuals results in the most articulated concept of society.

---

[30]Smith, *Moral Sentiments*, 44, 84.

[31]Smith, *Moral Sentiments*, 161-78.

[32]Smith, *Moral Sentiments*, 201-11.

[33]Smith, *Moral Sentiments*, 210.

Understanding society requires an attempt to understand fully the lives of its individuals. To understand concretely the cement and glue of a well-articulated society, one needs to capture the essence of the characters of the individuals who compose the society. It is important to understand the individuals' characters, not merely because they are intrinsically fascinating but because what an individual does in his or her societal life has deep implications for the lives of all individuals who live in the society. Thus individual A's conscious struggle to better himself to become friendly, affectionate, dutiful, self-commanding, modest, honest, beneficent, benevolent, courageous, self-respecting, and respectful of the humanity of others results not only in cultivating those necessary conditions of moral life, but by example encourages other individuals to do the same.[34] Every action that A undertakes has deep implications for the lives of B, C, and D.

I have indicated above that Smith's *The Wealth of Nations* and *The Theory of Moral Sentiments* may appear to be dealing with themes (political economy and morality) that seem to have no bearing on each other. Such a reading of Smith would be mistaken. Although Smith did not synthesize these, I think he intended to with the view of demonstrating the close relationship between morality and political economy. Clearly, a synthesis of the two dimensions would have compelled Smith to recognize the conflict between a moral theory based on the conceptions of humankind as capable of sympathy and a political economy which often resorts to the use of the unsocial sentiments particularly during periods in which capital accumulation and profit extraction are the chief goals of material progress. In practice, the result of such conflict is often a political economy that is willing to risk justice, morality, and the happiness of the greater number of people. Smith's economic whole resembles a full-fledged capitalist economy in which the individual's activities would not often pass the vigorous moral scrutiny of the *Theory of Moral Sentiments*. This result we may interpret as a consequence of at least three premises in Smith's theory:

---

[34]Smith, *Moral Sentiments*, 212-63.

1. Life itself is contradictory; therefore humankind's social and unsocial sentiments produced a divided self, a self that aspires to be moral by contributing to the happiness of society as a whole, and a self that is only willing to contribute to its individual happiness and sacrifice others. Therefore, the divided self reflects the constitution of human nature

2. Human nature is deeply affected by custom, habit, and education. If a society is not to collapse, a responsible government ought to reverse and ameliorate the divided self's unconscious problems

3. Humankind's unsocial sentiments can be harmonized carefully with the social sentiments and the result would be a society consisting of a basically well-to-do majority and a not very happy minority

In short, there is a fascinating tension in Smith's theories of moral ideals and pragmatic political economy. Ricardo inherits Smith's moral world but his concerns were essentially economic problems, which he did not fully solve. It is precisely the tensions in Smith and the problematic of the measure of value in Ricardo that set the stage for Marx.[35]

Rawls' Conceptions of Justice and Moral Order

> Whether justice as fairness can be extended to a general political conception for different kinds of societies existing under different historical and social conditions, or whether it can be extended to a general moral conception, or a significant part thereof are altogether separate questions. I avoid prejudging these larger questions one way or the other.[36]

Rawls wrote his seminal book, *A Theory of Justice*, with the implicit purpose of putting his own house (the American

---

[35]Smith, *Moral Sentiments*, 265-342.

[36]John Rawls, "Justice as Fairness: Political not Metaphysical," *Philosophy and Public Affairs* 14/3 (1985): 225.

democratic regime) in order. His book is guided by a political as opposed to a metaphysical conception of justice. Rawls propounds two principles which could serve as arbiters of divisive and controversial issues of justice that by and large characterize modern democratic regimes.

His principles can be extended to form a theory of justice incorporating political, cultural, and traditional diversities to the non-Western world as well. By modifying his ideas we may follow the spirit but not the letter of Rawls' conception of justice. By conceiving the self as metaphysical rather than political we may work out the outlines of a theory of morality and political economy or a theory of justice which specifically addresses the perennial themes of famine, hunger, and political justice as they characterize the African human condition.

Rawls' first statement of his two principles of justice said that (1) each person is to have an equal right to the most extensive basic liberty compatible with a similar liberty of others and (2) social and economic inequalities are to be arranged so that they are both (a) reasonably expected to be to everyone's advantage, and (b) attached to positions and offices open to all.[37] Subsequently, Rawls modified these principles as follows:

1. Each person has an equal right to a fully adequate scheme of equal basic rights and liberties, which scheme is compatible with a similar scheme for all

2. Social and economic inequalities are to satisfy two conditions: first, they must be attached to offices and positions open to all under conditions of fair equality of opportunity; and second, they must be to the greatest benefit of the least advantaged members of society[38]

Rawls himself has stated that his theory of justice was intended not as a general theory of the human condition, but rather it reflected upon deep inequalities within American

---

[37]John Rawls, *A Theory of Justice* (Cambridge: The Belknap Press of Harvard University Press, 1971), 60.

[38]Rawls, "Justice as Fairness," 227.

democratic society. It was intended as a critical liberal response to the deep inequalities generated by slavery in American political culture. We may distort Rawls' provisions and argue that the second principle can be applied just as easily to the political, social, and particularly economic injustices generated by colonialism and economic exploitation under market economies in all of the industrially underdeveloped parts of the world. The second principle is applicable to the deep inequalities (political, social, and economic) in Africa, particularly in those parts of Africa where hunger, poverty (prevalent in at least twenty-two African countries), and political repressions prevail.

If the second principle is to be applied to the African human condition it must be revised considerably along lines that Rawls might not allow. The second principle does not consider the crucial sense in which a market economy through systematic exploitation, as Marx argued, distorts an individual's life prospects by indirectly rendering some individuals dependent upon others for their livelihood. The market does this by wage labor. In Africa this system of wage labor was directly and indirectly applied to guarantee cheap labor and minerals from the continent, a system which in due course produced deep inequalities among the African populace. The deep inequalities in African societies (particularly among the landless African peasants and poor city dwellers) are related to the well-to-do inhabitants of technological, industrial societies.

Given the distorting function of a market economy in the African context, what is needed is a moral and political economic analysis of the interconnections between the deep inequalities in Africa and the materially comfortable life among the rich classes of modern industrial technological societies. Thus the discourse between thinkers arguing from the standpoint of the poor and the hungry in Africa and from the standpoint of both rational/moral thought and pragmatic/rational thought must not be on the plane of what the rich and comfortable should give to the poor. Rather the discourse should focus on (a) how the rich and the comfortable have indirectly contributed through an alienated and exploitative market economy to the generation of deep inequalities; (b) the psychological, moral, and economic consequences of these deep inequalities and how these affect the personalities of both the rich and comfortable on the one hand and the poor and

115

the hungry on the other; and (c) the need to find certain fundamental principles of justice which, by specifically addressing the peculiar African human condition, define the relationships between morality and political economy in a universally compelling manner.

Rawls' two principles fail to capture adequately the human essence of the African condition. We must develop further principles which address (a) the traditional cultural experiences of Africa and (b) the deep inequalities conditioned by the "morally unjust" experience of slavery, colonialism, and most recently of an alienating world market penetration of African economic systems. In one sense, (b) resembles the second part of Rawls' second principle of justice.

The new theory of morality and political economy which I develop here ultimately appeals to the potential educability of the human mind. The human self is capable of discovering moral rules even in institutions where they are only implicit. Such rules are not even implicit in our political traditions; they have to be newly constructed. The people who construct them sometimes will have to violate the "sacred codes" of prejudice in the authority of tradition.

4

THE AFRICAN CONCEPTION OF A
MORAL POLITICAL ECONOMY

From the previous discussion, we may say that classical political economy does not have an explicit theory of development and progress as moral and rational concepts. Rather, development and progress are viewed as material concepts requiring no guidance by rational moral principles internalized by authentic human beings. In contrast, traditional African social practices implicitly provide moral and rational views of progress and development. Indeed, it is true that development and progress are moral and rational concepts. Husserl's conceptions of the prescientific notion of the life-world is strikingly similar to the traditional prescientific African views of external nature, embedded in the natural life-world.

The African concept of the authentic human being is moral/rational as is the African concept of external nature. The African concept of the authentic human being has been deeply influenced by the traditional Africans' view of progress and development. In Africa, these activities have been constrained by the moral/rational view of the authentically human. Africans have refrained from objectifying external nature because it is sacred and dignified. One consequence of this respect for external nature is that modern science and technology has not completely transformed it. External nature was not emptied of its intrinsic moral dignity. Thus, progress and development still retain their hidden moral rational status. Among Africans they are not considered to be exclusively economic as they are in industrial society.

Human beings tend to identify with the part of the world they call home. Regions outside of their immediate horizon become negligible or alien. When we think abstractly, we tend to think of a particular region to which we were born and within which we grew, as the most important part of the world. The particular takes the place of the universal. The experiences and conditions of human beings outside of that particular region influence the particular to conceive of itself as the true universal. When the focus on the particular region reaches the apogee of dogmatism, nonthinking reaches a point of explosion. At that point, the bonds that potentially unite us in different particular regions as human beings give way to the differences that deeply divide us.

If we apply this reasoning to underdevelopment in Africa, we will conclude that underdevelopment can be overcome only if people in the industrial countries (region A) are willing to gear their social passions to sympathize with the human conditions in Africa (region B).

Progress and Development as Moral Concepts

The appeal to the moral capacity of region A to participate in the affairs of region B ultimately is based on a moral obligation. It is an appeal to reason combined with morality, which, as L. Wittgenstein put it remarkably well, compels the moral rational human being to choose "a road which everybody on seeing it would, with logical necessity, have to go, or be ashamed for not going." The recognition by A of its indirect, almost unnoticeable participation in the problems of region B may lead A to undertake action, which if not undertaken quickly could explode the volatile human situation in region B. An example of a region which continues to interact on this level is South Africa. Others exist among rich and poor Africans, and between rich and poor Africans and non-Africans.

The concept of development emerged from discussions of progress. This concept grew out of the debates and arguments concerning science around the beginning of the seventeenth century in Europe. The concept of development then is grounded upon the concept of progress; progress is in fact the necessary condition of material as opposed to nonmaterial development. The term progress was a controversial term among the writings of philosophers of science, sociologists, and economists. Thomas Hobbes in the seventeenth century, Smith in the eighteenth century, Emmannuel Kant, Hegel, and Marx in the nineteenth century have directly or indirectly commented on the concept of progress.

In the vast literature on progress, however, nowhere is the term precisely defined. Often progress as a material concept is lumped together with the nonmaterial aspect of progress. More often, progress is treated not only as a noun but as an adjective; thus a given idea is progressive as opposed to retrogressive. Rarely is an idea conceived as being both progressive and retrogressive with one dominating the other. Nor are the material and nonmaterial aspects of progressive and retrogressive ideas distinguished. These characteristics apply as well to the concept of development.

Husserl's Natural Attitude and its Implications for Progress and Development as Moral Concepts

Civilizations such as those in Egypt, Ethiopia, Mali, Senegal, Yoruba, and Mozambique existed long before the Greek polis and had a mode of discourse which may be characterized as natural or prescientific. The cultures that flowered later—particularly after the science of Gallileo and Newton—and the elements of natural thinking (the natural attitude of Edmund Husserl), may be summarized as follows.[1] According to Husserl, the natural attitude is the attitude that preceded the scientific world of Gallileo and Descartes.[2] The worlds of the Hebrews, the Greeks, and the Africans in one way or another were immersed in the natural prescientific attitude. The natural attitude is the world of religion broadly understood as myths, superstitions, customs, habits, unquestioned values, norms, and belief systems. Unlike the scientific world, a world of mathematical formulas, theorems, laws, axioms, and technical instruments, the prescientific world is as yet unknown. It is a world of rich appearances which is understood through dogma. It is known in the sense that it is dogmatically assumed to exist and unknown in the sense that its scientific penetration does not completely disclose its inner being. In that sense, the prescientific world is partly known and unknown.

The knowing subjects, like the object of their knowledge, the world itself, find themselves in the middle of this partly known and unknown world. The knowing subject also is partly known and

---

[1]Edmund Husserl, *The Crisis of European Sciences* (Evanston: Northwestern University Press, 1970).

[2]Husserl, *Crisis*, 50.

119

partly unknown to itself. The knowing subject is elusive to itself; it too is an unknown horizon. The knower and the world to-be-known are both unknown. The world as understood by the scientific attitude is as much unknowable as the world when taken for granted by the natural attitude's silence implicit in religion, common sense, and custom. Of course, science claims superiority over the prescientific attitude in that it attempted to study the vague natural world of stones, animals, minerals, air, and water, and give a precise, predictable account of the nature of these objects as well as the nature of the human beings that work on nature. In so doing, the scientific attitude thinks it has transcended the prescientific or natural attitude.

The natural world is comprehended by the power of intuition in the natural attitude. The scientific attitude comprehends phenomena scientifically; the natural attitude intuits the world. The ultimate struggle in the quest for understanding the world is then between comprehension and intuition. Intuition leaves us with vaguely but richly perceived human experiences, witchcraft, religions, and aesthetic experiences that are never directly replicable. They do not repeat themselves and they cannot be inductively manipulated. There is a dimension of mystery and darkness to these experiences that cannot be experienced visually or comprehended intellectually. That which intuition fails to do but which the scientific attitude chooses to do is precisely to leave the hidden as hidden, to leave the unexposable unexposed, to be silent before the unspeakable.

The scientific attitude consciously struggles to capture the complex natural world in a net of ideas, that is in a net of symbolic mathematical theories. It is only the scientifically knowable world that is the world for the scientist. As a scientist, one can forget oneself and one's own unknowability once one loses oneself in the fabricated world of mathematical theories. The prescientific African peasant does not think in mathematical theories. For the most part, similar to peasants in the early phases of the European world, African peasants still have a prescientific attitude.

The natural (prescientific) attitude and the scientific attitude toward development are radically different. Development for the scientific attitude is the ability with which humans materially transform the natural world. The human subject for a given nation of subjects that transformed its world along the path of first discovering science along with technology and then applying the know-how to cultivate its world in the sense of feeding, clothing, and housing is materially developed. Such a human subject or nation has overcome the material burden of life of all its citizens. According to a strict interpretations of material development, there is not a nation in the world that presently is materially developed. According to both the strict and loose interpretations of material development of the scientific attitude, material development is an ideal that no human subject or a nation of subjects has yet realized. It is time that we faced this fact and strive to realize material development.

The scientific attitude, strictly understood, is also an ideal. It too seems to be an unrealized ideal. Nature in all its complexity is not yet comprehended fully by the penetrating power of the scientific attitude. In this sense, the scientific attitude is also a participant in the prescientific attitude which, according to Husserl, it seems not to be able to transcend. External nature, Husserl assures us, will always remain external to the knowing subject; part of external nature will remain hidden, will refuse total transformation by the power of scientific reasoning. It is the task of the scientific attitude, however, to strive to overcome the resistance. The project of material development is one aspect of a dogged striving of the scientific attitude to overcome the silent resistance of external nature to yield to humankind's aspiration and desires for the good life free of the absence of basic material necessities: food, clothing, and shelter.

Dasein (the human), according to Heidegger, who was profoundly influenced by Husserl, is a meaning giver.[3] Everything that the world possesses is given a peculiarly human meaning by humankind in the quest for truth, the quest for finding one's place in the world of things as envisioned by the world. Dasein has "a natural inclination and privilege to give meaning to reality."[4] As a meaning giver, as a symbol interpreter, Dasein is unavoidably bound by time, culture, history, contexts, situations, prepositions, prejudices, and tradition. These above elements invariably color Dasein's meaning—giving activity; under their powerful influence,

---

[3]For an illuminating interpretation of Heidegger as applicable to the possibility of the founding of African philosophy, see Theophilus O'Kere, *African Philosophy: A Historico-Hermeneutical Investigation of the Conditions of Its Possibility* (New York: University Press of America, 1983), 32-54.

[4]O'Kere, *African Philosophy*, 54.

Dasein nakedly encounters its finitude. Every human meaning then is ultimately an interpretation of life within the framework of the human's finitude. Humans are finite. They give meanings to their existence from the perspective of their time, culture, history, contexts, situation, prepositions, prejudices, and traditions. Consequently, human beings are hermeneutical creatures.

Development and Prescientific Culture in Africa

In the prescientific African world, as in the Western world of scientific attitude, the activity of meaningfully interpreting one's world is especially affected by Dasein's historicity, in particular Dasein's finitude. The African self also understands its world from its culture. The African prescientific attitude gives a moral/rational meaning to development. The prescientific attitude, as Husserl and Heidegger contend, is one in which the world is interpreted meaningfully; the meanings are uncovered by symbols, myths, religion, and art. The understanding of the life-world is precisely the understanding of the symbols, myths, religion, and art as life forms. These life forms are inhabited by the life-world, and the life-world itself is taken as a natural phenomenon of a complex but ultimately coherent structure of meaning and purpose. It is, however, a world which traditional Africans have already inter-preted and taken for granted. It is a world which makes sense and gives a stable orientation to the subjective world of its inhabitants. It is from within its already interpreted and structured world, from within its culturally lived language and signs that the inhabitants understand their world. It is a world in which the authority of tradition and human prejudice penetrate deeply. In this sense, the prescientific attitude is immersed in the unwillingness to question dispassionately and reflect upon its prejudices and judgments, and liberate itself from tradition. This refusal to radically dismantle the hold which the authority of tradition has on the prescientific attitude is one of the many features of the life-world as Husserl understands it.

Economically, the African prescientific attitude of nature does not lead to natural progress. There are communities in Africa that refuse to clear forests which are crucial for agriculture. From an economic standpoint, such behavior is irrational; it directly determines material underdevelopment. From the viewpoint of the prescientific attitude, the horizon of the life-world when the life-world is dogmatically and nonreflectively internalized, the above

122

behavior shows a reverence for a nature which a higher force designed. To clear the forest, the people might argue, is to destabilize the order of nature; to challenge, however vainly, the authority of the creator who intended that forests satisfy our aesthetic needs for beauty or the need to worship in the wilderness of nature.

The prescientific attitude is a complex, structured whole composed of self-validating internal rules. The rules themselves govern behavior not so much because they are "right," but because they work rather well in that they enable the participants to live a predictably stable life, the ideal of all communities. Communities want the dependability of behavior which is gained from the accumulation of laws gleaned from experience, and the accumulation of the rightness and wrongness of these laws. The process of discovery is by and large inductive insofar as the authority of experience is crucial to the accumulation of knowledge. We might say, life in the prescientific society is not experienced as a series of hypotheses; life there is experienced as that which always has been and always shall be. One important feature of the life-world is that it is a world of myths and beliefs. The refusal to clear the forest exemplifies material underdevelopment.

From the standpoint of culture, the way of life in the prescientific society is resistant to internal criticism. The participants' explanation according to Western economics leads to nonprogress. Therefore, it is antiprogress. For the economists, it renders material civilization impossible, which ultimately means that the African world view is unscientific and primitive when juxtaposed with the scientific spirit. Are the scientists right in their judgments of the prescientific attitude?

I have already characterized a feature of the life-world as that of a world filled with superstition, unexamined beliefs, and dogmatically internalized world views. Husserl has contended "consciously, we always live in the life-world."[5] By this statement he means that the scientist and the nonscientist, the scientific attitude and the prescientific attitude, ultimately are anchored upon the life-world; the world of prejudices, superstitions, unexamined beliefs, and dogmatically internalized world views. In this specialized sense, both the prescientific and scientific attitudes

---

[5]Husserl, *Crisis*, 379.

have no way by which they could escape the penetration of prejudice, superstition, unexamined beliefs, and dogmatically internalized world views. The individual man or woman is inserted into an already structured world. It itself is simply the world. The individual examines from the given, existent tradition of the closed life-world; he or she is conscious of the world as a horizon. Furthermore, the individual experiences the life-world as its life-world; the life-world may be given to humankind as a whole, but it is experienced by each person as his or her world. The life-world is an arena of human interests which are experienced as particular interests by so many human types. The life-world thus is collectively inhabited but it is individually experienced. Each member of the life-world undertakes an individual task, a particular project, has a distinct goal. These, however, are done in a communal context. It appears as if each individual is consciously following a particular path that is intended to fill the whole vessel. The relationship of the various individuals is that they are bound to each other and to the world by an invisible communal bond.

The scientific thinkers, who use a specialized theoretical language in their definition of their various tasks, in their thematic understanding of the life-world in the end essentially do what the prescientific thinkers do in their intuitive understanding of the life-world. In a magnificent passage, Husserl writes,

> Pre-given nature—the domain of the life-world-corpored nature—[is that] which is familiar to the ordinary man in everyday life and which he can get to know "in more detail" but which he simply has no reason to single out and consider in a coherent way in its abstract unitary character, as natural science proposes to do. For [the scientist], it is the pre-given sphere of being for which he wishes to accomplish something new: theory for nature, theoretically true being, predictive determination under the idea of unconditionally, universally valid truth.[6]

Furthermore,

---

[6]Husserl, *Crisis*, 382.

The life-world is the world that is constantly pre-given, valid constantly and in advance as existing, but not valid because of some purpose of investigation, according to some universal end. Every end presupposes it; even the universal end of knowing it in scientific truth presupposes it, and in advance; and in the course of (scientific) work, it presupposes it ever anew, as a world existing, in its own [to be sure] but existing nevertheless.[7]

The Superiority of the Prescientific Attitude

The life-world to the prescientific human being, such as the traditional African, is a world of stones, air, animals, tools, plants, and minerals. In a very unscientific way—that is, without theoretical science: biology, physics, or chemistry—the stones, air, animals, tools, plants, and minerals are intimately known to the human beings who appropriate them. Their knowledge of nature's entities, however, lacks the sophistication and clarity of external nature as captured through the biologist's microscope, the physicist's telescope, and the chemist's analyses. What the prescientific mind struggles to know with the naked eye, the unaided hands, the scientific mind strives to know through the aid of techniques and technologies. The partial knowledge of nature as experienced by the prescientific mind is supplemented by the scientific mind's equally partial knowledge. In both instances, however, nature is inadequately known, although the inadequacies are markedly different. In the end, however, both the scientific mind and prescientific mind ground what each knows inadequately to their intuitive grasp of the world as a "given" of the pregiven existence of the life-world. Both minds ultimately respond to an already coherently structured world of stones, air, animals, tools, plants, and minerals.

Earlier I contended that the concept of progress in its technical, economic, and spiritual dimensions is conceived by the scientific mind as progressive when compared with the prescientific conception. The concept of development too is significantly intertwined with the concept of progress. That which is conceived as progressive is implied to be developed. In the

---

[7]Husserl, *Crisis*, 387.

concept of development, as with the concept of progress, the technical, economic, and spiritual dimensions are rarely distinguished from each other. This issue raises some significant problems.

What is development? If the discussion of the life-world from Husserl's standpoint is sufficiently convincing to serve as a framework within which the prescientific and scientific attitudes may be examined, then the concepts of development and progress acquire a unique place. The framework has enough complexity to challenge our conventional understandings of what development entails. The life-world, we learn from Husserl, is a world in which human beings in their capacity as scientific and prescientific thinkers are rooted. Human beings are born into the world as it is. They have the capacity to change within that world by revising and critically appropriating the social practices of that world in its pregiven form. Its pregiveness is embodied in the social practices that initially do not allow critical questioning of habits, customs, beliefs, religion, or superstitions. Indeed, some of these social practices are regarded as so sacred that they serve as authorities which cannot be challenged.

The social practice of the sacredness of forests provides a classical illustration of one of the many aspects of the life-world. This practice is on the one hand a dimension of development when development is understood as a spiritual habit of the mind; it is regarded as a dimension of underdevelopment when development is considered a technical and economic-social practice.

Africans need food, shelter, and clothing. Human beings work external nature's trees, woods, stones, and cottons to provide their basic needs. Some Africans, however, have refused to cut trees in order to preserve the sublimity of the forests, from which is drawn a mystical vision of life. The vision is deep and worthy of our respect. Equally worthy is the obligation to our human body for food, warmth, and shelter. The mystical vision of life tends to have a reductionistic conception of the soul. Its spirituality often denies the recognition of the body's needs. The body's hunger for food in our example is denied by the refusal to cut trees. Authentic spirituality, however, requires us to satisfy our bodily and nonbodily needs. Africans must recognize their duty to adequately feed, clothe, and shelter themselves. Genuine development is both spiritual and material. Those Africans who deny the body would be well advised to rethink their position and come to realize that since they cannot remove the body, they have to feed it. Therefore, they must develop human technologies which would allow them to transform nature so as to self-sufficiently provide their bodily needs.

The spiritually admirable refusal to cut trees in precolonial Africa is economically unintelligent. It is this mode of thinking that led some people to put underdevelopment upon the shoulders of Africans by saying that Africans were backward, uninnovative, and lazy. A reasonable African must not refuse to cut the trees, but should insist that there is a sensitive way of cutting trees. This way requires the service of sensitive technology that is respectful of external nature. Neither the scientific world nor Africa has developed such technology. Instead, both the scientific and prescientific proponents of development remain in their one-sided horizons. Thus, the scientific mind has little justification to consider such a social practice as manifestly a case of under-development; "development" is an ambiguous word, and we are advised to use it cautiously.

The scientific mind, however, may be justified in reducing the concept of development to its technical and economic aspects in the years after the world began to develop industrially and *homo economicus* became the ideal of the materially civilized life. Socrates[8] consciously rejected economic man as a possible ideal, whereas modernity has fully embraced him.[9]

When men and women thusly regard themselves as homo economicus, their concepts of development and progress become deeply affected by the domination of the hegemonic idea, by the idea that economic worth is the primary and ultimate worth. This domination in turn leads to the suppression of the spiritual

---

[8]See in particular Allan Bloom, ed., *The Republic of Plato* (Basic Books: New York, London, 1968). There is an illuminating discussion of the limitations of happiness acquired from a materially rich life, and the type of happiness that comes from the righteously lived life. The philosophic life has the potentiality to show those who are immersed in the life of material gains the path toward the genuinely happy life. See the first ten pages of Book IV of *The Republic of Plato*. The ideal of antiquity was the righteous or just person; the challenge was precisely to know what righteousness and justice are.

[9]For a discussion of these themes, see Hannah Arendt, *The Human Condition* (Chicago: The University of Chicago Press, 1958), 79-126, 248-329.

meaning of development by the glittering presence of the technical and economic meanings of progress. In such a world, the world of technology, humankind's ideal is technical and economic development. The spiritual meaning of development is openly declared "primitive," "retrogressive," "prescientific." In Husserl's terms, the life-world as such, and particularly the life-world's anti-modern "core" structure, its solid pregiveness, is rejected by modernity as romantic and antiprogress, unworthy of serious attention. The life-world's core structure is something that science cannot penetrate. If it cannot be penetrated, so the argument runs, it cannot be rationalized or carefully quantified and measured. It is therefore irrational, if it cannot be quantified and measured, and it is impossible to subject it to verifiable propositions. The objects of nature—stones, air, plants, animals, and minerals—can become the subjects of human discourse if and when they are quantifiable, analyzable, measurable. Otherwise, these objects of nature are, materially speaking, useless in that in their passive form they serve no purpose for development in the technical and economic sense. The objects of nature are of course useful for poetic discourse and religious experience. But those spiritual functions are precisely what modernity's specialized notion of development cannot understand.

The concept of economic man has become the ideal of much of humankind, an ideal that attempts to realize itself in scientific discourse. Science is the accepted language of modernity's citizens. The life-world's core structure, which has its own language of poetry, parables, and myths, resists a precise proposi-tional form; its languages often are dismissed hastily by the scientific attitude as undiscussable, unredeemable. Ultimately it is because of the above prejudice that the social practices of the nonindustrial world, of which Africa is an example, are judged as "primitive" and the result of "closed mentalities." Jurgen Habermas has stated this prejudice in his *Theory of Communicative Action* as follows:

> Winch holds that it is illegitimate to press the demand for consistency further than the Azande of themselves do; he comes to the conclusion "that it is the European, obsessed with pressing Zande thought where it would not naturally go—to a contradiction—who is guilty of misunderstanding, not the Azande. The European is in fact committing a category

mistake." A belief in witches ought not to be confused with a quasi-theory; for the Azande do not intend with it to comprehend processes in the world in the same objectivating attitude as does a modern physicist or a physician trained in the natural sciences.

The charge of a category mistake raised against the European anthropologist can be understood in a strong and in a weak sense. If it says merely that the scientist should not impute to the natives his own interest in resolving inconsistencies, the question naturally arises, whether this lack of a theoretical interest may not be traced back to the fact that the Zande world view imposes less exacting standards of rationality than the modern understanding of the world.[10]

If the criteria of what constitutes development and progress are changed from the exclusively economic model to the rational/moral model, traditional Africa's views of the self or nature have substantial insights to offer to contemporary moral philosophy. One of the lessons that one could learn from traditional Africa's prescientific attitude toward nature is that there is a profound tension between the conception of the human being and the rational/moral conception. This tension is reflected in the statements of some leading moral philosophers and economists.

Consider, for example, Smith's view that music is useless because economically speaking it is unproductive of capital. Therefore, the musician's trade is useless for economic growth. The musician contributes nothing to the accumulation of capital. For Smith, the musician is indeed a worker, but not a worker who produces capital, and therefore not really a worker in the strict economic sense. Smith misses a crucial point about the nature and goal of music, and consequently the role of the musician in any society. That the musician is an unproductive worker and that production is only capital oriented is a view of a very narrow mind—a charge of which Smith cannot easily be proven guilty—and misunderstands the nature of music, and the role of the musician.

---

[10]Jurgen Habermas, *The Theory of Communicative Action* vol. 1 (Boston: Beacon Press, 1981), 60-61.

Music, as in the ancient Greek and African civilizations, is designed to introduce the ideal of harmony in the human being's soul. The harmonious human is open to seeing and hearing foreign thoughts and ideas that it would otherwise refuse to consider. Good music seeks to exercise the delicate task of the cognitive, rational, moral, and emotional instruction of human beings. The consciously chosen task assigned by Smith to the activity of music then is not the production of capital, but rather the difficult task of rational, moral education of the human soul. Therefore, the task of the musician, as was true in the ancient African cultures during the precolonial era, is that of the educator. The African musician was a moral educator, an enlightener, a recollector of memories, a nostalgic singer, a melancholic but also joyous decipherer of stories, myths, and allegories. Sometimes he was a dreamer and a utopist. Clearly, moral education toward the best and the ideal, enlightening the illiterate through music by the subtle tools of storytelling and recollecting do not produce capital. The above tasks, some of which are done by critically conscious African musicians, require measurement with much loftier yard-sticks. Smith's narrow economic yardstick is simply inadequate to the important task of appraising both the nature of music and the role of the musician. The critical musician is a producer of love and brotherhood, friendship and concord, good will and under-standing.

African Philosophy and Underdevelopment

Africans and Africanists continue to discuss the question of African philosophy.[11] It is important for Africans to examine the

---

[11]For an excellent introduction to the topic see Paulin J. Hountondji, *African Philosophy* (Bloomington: Indiana University Press, 1983). Another African philosopher, Chukwudum B. Okilo, has recently advanced yet another working definition of philosophy, "a reasoned or critical reflection on the universe and man's place in it." From this definition he draws the conclusion that African philosophy is philosophical in the same sense. African philosophy is a reasoned and reflective activity. (*Quest*, 3/1 [June 1989]: 22). One of the best-known African philosophers is Placide Tempels. His book *Bantu Philosophy* (Paris: Prescence Africaine, 1949) is attacked by Hountondji for reducing the plurastic essence of philosophy in Africa to a single collective philosophy of the Bantus. For Hountondji, philosophy as such is a

question. The examination will be relevant to Africans if the pragmatic dimension of philosophizing is appreciated so that philosophy could then serve the needs of transforming and developing Africa. Philosophy as such is concretely useful if we can draw from it principles which can be used innovatively to guide the burning issues of life—food, shelter, clothing, freedom, and faith.

Paulin Hountondji was one of the first Africans to ask whether there was an African philosophy. The answer is a qualified yes, but the question needs some truly radical modification. He effectively argues that philosophy is not *ethnophilosophy* (Temples, Kagame). Nor is it the heightening of the emotive African soul (Césaire). By philosophy he understands

> a literature produced by Africans and dealing with philosophical problems. . . . African philosophy exists, but it is not what it is believed to be. It is developing objectively in the form of a literature rather than as implicit and collective thought, but as a literature of which the output remains captive to the unanimist fallacy.[12]

---

solitary, historical (not ontological), systematic, and creative activity that produces literate, critical, reflective literature by Africans who engage in philosophy. See also W.E. Abraham, *The Mind of Africa* (Chicago: University of Chicago Press, 1962). Other classic texts are Alexis Kagame's *La Philosophie Bantu-Rwandisse de L'Etre* (Bruxelles: Academie Royal du Science Colonial, 1956); and Kwame, *An Essay on African Philosophical Thought* (Cambridge: Cambridge University Press, 1987). For Paul Rordin, Africans philosophize in the following sense: "There can be little doubt that every human group, no matter how small, has, from time immemorial, contained individuals who were constrained by their individual temperaments and interests to occupy themselves with the basic problems of what we customarily term philosophy." See Paul Rordin, *Primitive Man As Philosopher* (New York: Dover, 1957), 21. The neglected work of Theophilus O'Kere, *African Philosophy*, deserves recognition. For O'Kere, African philosophy is practicable only as hermenuetics. Theophilus O'Kere, *African Philosophy* (New York: University Press of America, 1983).

[12]See Hountondji, *African Philosophy*, 63, 69.

This is a rather bold and controversial statement which I wish to examine within the context of the human condition in Africa.

What Hountondji has done to philosophy is provincially academic. To the extent that he thinks literature is restricted to writing and that one is a philosopher only if he or she writes, then one of the most authentic amd genuinely philosophical individuals, namely Socrates, is not a philosopher. Hountondji, the self-conscious philosopher, cannot denude Socrates of the very critical and reflective activity of philosophy which Socrates himself established. Furthermore, if philosophy is merely literature produced by academic philosophers, then all of the critical, meditative, and morally sensitive thinkers in prescientific Africa who never taught in universities are not philosophers. If Hountondji believes this, then he is wrong and he needs to reexamine the nature of philosophy.

Philosophy is not merely literature, but can include literature in the form of writing about what is wondered. Fundamentally, however, philosophy is not only what professional philosophers do, but is a universal activity which human beings engage in, as wonderers and thinkers, to examine themselves, and in an existentially serious way to seek to transform themselves and the world in which they exist. Philosophy then is an activity which an existentially serious person practices guided by critical and reflective principles, under the ever-present gaze of a reflective presence.

I concur, however, with Hountondji as well as Mudimbe (*The Invention of Africa*) when they say that the European conception of the other is deeply flawed. He cites as an example Tempel's conception of the Bantu as being essentially systematic, in its own way logical and ontological, an ontology that consists of "vital force" as opposed to the Christian Being as the ultimate mover. The chief flaw is that Africans are all put into one category and the self is collectivized. There is a disturbing lack of respect of the sovereignty and autonomy of the individual, solitary self. The absence of this respect disqualifies Tempel's view from being a philosophical work.

Philosophy is a very solitary activity, although the results of solitarily thought can have vital and transformative effects on the culture in which the thinkers live. I can think only by myself. When I think I do not think as an African, but rather as a solitary, wondering self—a self which could be perturbed by the material

132

and spiritual conditions in Africa, by its hunger, poverty, untimely death, starving children, and poor peasants. I think only to determine my destiny and to construct values and norms by which to guide my life.[13]

I think solitarily. The contents of my thoughts, however, are social. They come out of society. As such the social themes are living burdens of philosophy. When one understands philosophy as a solitary human activity, one can understand how Africans engaged in this activity in their relentless struggles to resist the enslaver, the colonizer, the imperialist. It is during such intense moments of suffering that philosophy is born. In this sense philosophy is born out of struggle.

In ancient Greece, philosophy produced Socrates, a gifted and solitary individual who provoked others to question the premises of their opinions. This bold, honest, and solitary thinker clearly showed the way of philosophizing. He did not produce literature, as Hountondji demands of philosophy. He instead injected philosophy into everyday life. Socrates maintained that all selves become authentic only when they seek to examine the way they live their lives, the way they take care of their fragile souls. With Socrates everyday life itself becomes philosophic. Not all individuals could write and thus produce philosophy as literature. But all individuals can sit and think. Philosophy is fundamentally a vehicle for thinking, and thinking is a fundamentally moral activity. It is an activity, contrary to Hountondji's assertion, in which all of us engage. Nor is philosophy as a moral activity merely a world view. It is more fluid, less dogmatic, and more unassuming than world views. It is an enterprise of perpetual questioning.

Philosophy as moral activity which is practiced by the existentially serious self may not produce literature. However, it can help society to awaken from the dangers of luxury, corruption, and comfort when it furnishes us with powerful, fresh, and self-regenerating principles. These principles could be deeply imbedded in the moral fibers of the solitary self and become effective habits. These habits could enable the self to realize that luxuries, corruption, and slavishness to money, unless carefully checked by principles, can give us a society haunted by hunger and

---

[13]Tedros Kiros, "Self-Determination," *The Journal of Social Philosophy* 22/1 (Spring 1991): 92-102.

a food crisis as is the case in Africa. Chapter 5 elaborates on what I mean by principles.

The question of African philosophy needs to be reevaluated in terms of philosophy's relevance to handle the facts of hunger, poverty, and underdevelopment as themselves expressions of *necessity*. Since the time of Aristotle, philosophers have sought to have philosophy in the form of practical wisdom handle the dimension of justice. Practical wisdom's obligation to everyday life is a central topic of Aristotle's *Nicomachean Ethics*. Contemporary philosophizing in Africa also should be practiced as practical wisdom and as humane pragmatism. Professional philosophers need to produce texts as relevant to the transformation of Africa as the celebrated work of Rawls', *A Theory of Justice*, is relevant to the American democratic system.

Unless African philosophy is rendered relevant to the human condition in Africa, it will devalue itself as an activity, as well as a discourse about the other. As Mudimbe has argued persuasively, the other is the invention of missionaries and ethnologists.[14] There is no African "other" as such who should patiently wait the discovery of a form of philosophy, an African philosophy that uniquely addresses him or her. Philosophy, as an activity propelled by principles and guided by the reflective presence, can contribute substantially to the question of Africa's desperate need to develop, by gently drawing Africans to participate willfully in the activity of thinking, of examining themselves and thereby ridding themselves of the corrupting and unnecessary luxuries which are draining the continent's dormant material resources.

There is no philosophy that uniquely addresses the African psyche, just as there exists no philosophy which addresses Europeans collectively. Philosophy is a universal discourse.[15] It is a classless activity, contrary to the way it has been practiced historically. It is a powerful generator of principles which mediate the need for justice, wisdom, equality, and liberty. It is as a

---

[14]See V.Y. Mudimbe, *The Invention of Africa* (Bloomington: Indiana University Press, 1988).

[15]This view is not popular among African philosophers. Again, as Mudimbe has shown, African philosophers have vacillated between those who defend a regionalization of rationalities and those who defend the universality of philosophy. See Mudimbe's *The Invention of Africa*, pp. 187-203.

generator of principles that philosophy is obligated to guide the great debate about hunger, poverty, and underdevelopment in Africa. The principles articulated in chapter 5 have the potential to truly overcome the crippling effects of colonialism and help Africans to initiate a new beginning, a new enlightenment which will never forget the past but instead will give the past a rich and spirited form of a radical present.

5

PHILOSOPHICAL PRINCIPLES FOR
AFRICAN DEVELOPMENT

Thinking and Morality

The self when it is seriously habituated can abide by internally generated principles that could simultaneously guide action and control behavior. The self as a moral/rational agent generates principles. In the context of African underdevelopment, we must ask, What are principles? Are human beings capable of generating principles? Why do Africans need principles? In what ways can principles contribute to the improvement of the human condition in Africa? By principles, I mean that human beings are capable of generating and cultivating highly general but practicable guidelines which guide their behavior, practices, and everyday existence. Once principles are formed, people may constantly refine and redefine them. The above statement serves as a working understanding of what I mean by principles.

Whether human beings are capable of generating principles is another matter. My response is yes. It is not a misreading of history to assert that human beings have argued and continue to argue both that there are definitive principles that ought to be good, valid, and binding for everyone, and that people deny the presence and their discovery of such principles. In the tradition of moral philosophy the former is moral absolutism and the latter nihilism. Discussion continues about the presence or absence of principles as such. If it is true that the history of human beings has included a struggle over the presentation and denial of principles then it follows that modern human beings are indeed capable of being generators of self-constructed principles. What is true of the historical past continues to be true of the present. Therefore, the quest for the founding of principles is a living project. The African poor are capable of generating principles that may enable them to address the issues of poverty, hunger, and senseless wars. They need to found an African ethical sub-community within a potentially binding world ethical community.

A response to the query whether Africans need principles is contained in the previous two paragraphs. There, however, I attempted to deal with the conception of principles as such, and the capacity and will of human beings to be guided consistently by coherently designed principles, when principles are understood as self-generated and with which human beings freely choose to habituate themselves. Africans, as much as other human beings, are in need of principles. Certain principles, carefully generated, might be capable of guiding responses to the questions of deep inequalities in economic, social, and political life in modern African countries, and to the lack of food.

At present Africa is characterized by the conspicuous presence of poverty, hunger, senseless wars, and incompetent and alienated elites. These characteristics are partly the legacies of slavery, colonialism, and neocolonialism, and partly attributable to the African conception of the self and external nature. Chapter 2 sheds light on the causes of African material underdevelopment. The subsequent two chapters contributed toward the resolution of the problem of material underdevelopment by appealing to the implicit moral sensibilities of those who presently possess the technological know-how with which some rudimentary issues of poverty and hunger could be addressed. This ideal conceivably could happen if certain principles of justice were adopted and if human beings choose to deliberate about the human condition in Africa from the standpoint of principles. The adoption of principles which make moral and political sense is worth pursing. Human beings can see the need of principles for the sake of living the life of peace, justice, and freedom. They may reason that peace, justice, and freedom are values that have a profound meaning in their everyday lives, and that the way of principles may be one desirable way with which to bring about an ethical community.

In what ways can principles contribute to the improvement of the human condition in Africa? Two indispensable principles are apparent, that of the inalienability of food for those who need it and that of the ending of senseless wars, giving rise to peace and

137

freedom. These are grounded on what we may term *continental thinking*. This way of thinking would allow Africans to strive for solutions to national and regional problems in Africa by mobilizing continental resources that are distributed unevenly throughout the continent. The elites of Africa should look beyond their particular concerns and act from the standpoint of principles that apply in a reasonable and human way to the conditions of the poor African peasantry, the potential human sources of material and spiritual civilization. Continental thinking would be no more than an empty phrase were it not carefully explicated. One careful explication requires understanding the nature of thinking itself.

Thinking is a distinctively moral activity. By thinking, I mean what ordinarily we do not mean. When person A asks person B the question, "What are you doing?" the other simply replies, "I am thinking." For person B thinking may mean any of the following. It might imply

1.   that a person was shocked by something he saw, for example a homeless person, and reflects on what he might do to help that person
2.   calculating what must be done, for example, how much profit should one make from a business
3.   figuring out the hidden aspects of a person's behavior, for example, what did my boss mean?
4.   intently concentrating on something such as looking at an artwork
5.   wondering or meditating, say on the structure of the university
6.   recollection, that is, remembering a past experience

There is, however, another level of thinking, that is moral thinking, which ought to be added on to the six implications of thinking that are current in our tradition of moral philosophy. Thinking is an activity that is guided by reason and stimulated by the depth of the feeling of the human spirit. It is an activity that houses both the mind and the spirit, and in which both play an equal part. When thinking is understood as a moral activity, it then becomes possible to prevent nonmoral activities (such as robbing from a poor person) arising out of thinking such as calculating profit mentioned above. Individuals who consciously

138

engage in thinking as a moral activity consciously avoid immoral activities.

Thinking is a moral activity in yet another way: it is invariably connected with the phenomenon of caring. Caring and thinking about others are intimate neighbors. Indeed, any person who engages in thinking cannot help but be involved in thinking about others, including unknown others. It is authentic thinking that gently but firmly convinces others deliberately to cultivate their minds and hearts to habituate themselves to the virtuous activity of caring. Caring then is guided by profound authentic thinking, which is both reasonable and moral rather than mindless emotionalism.

The most difficult form of thinking is to think about the human condition using self-imposed principles as guides to think about other human beings whom we cannot directly see and to whom we cannot directly speak. Thinking in the African context can take the food crisis as a focus. Although thinking and caring are intimate neighbors, thinking about others in a conscious manner is an exceedingly difficult moral activity. Why should we think about unseen others, for example the victims of the food crisis in Africa? Should not all those "others" think about themselves? These are not easy questions to answer.

When profoundly moved by the daily account of how those "others" are living, the humanly best response I am capable of is either despair, passive anger, or sympathy. These three forms of response of course are dignified in themselves, particularly when they are compared with other common forms of response such as indifference, or a cold refusal to be affected.

Indifference, callousness, refusal to be affected by the plight of others have been socially accepted forms of response since the days of antiquity. The authentic self of our tradition of modernity is a self that is deliberately emptied of any moral characteristic. The modern Western image of the ideal person generally seems to be one which is proudly practical, power centered, and self-motivated. It is always possible that there may be individuals whose observable behavior is not an honest and complete expression of their whole being. There undoubtedly exist individuals who choose not to show their real selves and are consequently always concealed behind the web of appearance. In such a case,

139

a problem arises from our hasty portrayal of the self within the apparent framework of modernity's culture.

The existence of certain sympathetic and compassionate individuals who hide their goodness from others and justify their behavior by religious convictions presents no unsurmountable problem. Not all individuals think about others in public. Indeed, the moment that goodness is practiced to attract the attention and praise of others, the good work immediately loses its profundity; it cheapens itself. It is in the nature of goodness that it be exercised without self-exposure. Authentically good people do work which does not disclose themselves. Such people who think about others in a nonpublic way and are ideal human types who already are doing the dutiful work which self-imposed principles would foster. Whatever the individuals' explanations or justifications of their dutiful behavior, we cannot fail to admire them as exemplary. Thus, the existence of individuals who practice goodness unostentatiously demonstrates to us that thinking about others is not difficult. On the contrary, there are exemplary individuals who happily seem to do good. Such individuals are our models; they inspire us.

Such individuals are the types, following Smith's *Theory of Moral Sentiments*, who have a capacity for justice. They have a sense of justice which is visible through their abilities to sympathize and live with other points of view. Such individuals genuinely cry and laugh with unknown others; they have a rare ability to make others' griefs and joys their own. We may envy their goodness as natural to them, and despair of achieving it ourselves. If we were to delve deeply into the backgrounds of these people, their family upbringing, education, religious convictions, and so forth, we might penetrate the source of their "natural goodness." We might find that their behavior was in fact unnatural instead. We would have understood the disciplined struggle which these people underwent in the training and education of their impulses by the gentle power of reason.

These exemplary individuals have stories to tell. Their virtuous behavior and good moral characteristics were not easy to come by. These virtues required years of self-discipline, self-control, and self-education. The individuals submitted their impulses, often undisciplined passions, and desires to the restraint, discipline, and limits of self-generated principles. Such principles are part of self-education toward freedom. Freedom seduces without force invites us gently. By analogy, the restraining power of self-generated and self-imposed principles is not coercive; rather it is a tempting invitation toward another way of life, another mode of being in the world. The possibility of freedom, a new way of being in the world, is always available for human beings to embrace, provided that they think about the need of being free, and that they struggle to be free. It is ultimately a matter of choice, a radical existential choice combined with a resolve to pursue the choice. Agnes Heller has written,

> In order to choose among sets of norms rather than merely entering pre-existing ones, in other words, in order to commit ourselves to norms and actions by virtue of moral reasons, we must first choose ourselves as persons who are ready to examine norms and actions from a moral point of view, as persons who give the moral point of view preference to any other (pragmatic) reasons. Following Kierkegaard, I mean by existential choice the choice of the very choice between good and evil. The existential choice is not introduced here as an ontological category, but rather as a historical one.
>
> If norms and values are relatively coherent, the value-orientation "good and evil" has priority over all other orienting values ("good comes first"), and everyone knows what good is. The norms are external to the individual, they are normally embedded in meaningful, legitimate world-views and there is no choice between norms, except during periods of crisis, even if norms are eventually open to interpretation.
>
> However, if we choose the choice between good and evil, we have already chosen the good, for if we make an existential choice, if we choose between good and evil, then we have chosen ourselves as honest

persons, as ones who give priority to moral reasons over other reasons.[1]

Throughout this chapter, I will make her arguments my own; however, I will pay more attention to the discussion of self-generated principles, following both Kant[2] and Hegel[3] in this particular regard. My argument is that once the existential choice is made, what the chooser needs are certain basic principles combined with systematically and collectively cultivated human institutions: a constitution, responsible social organizations, participatory political institutions, "objective" educational settings, each of which is guided by the self-generated principles of the choosers that inhabit the institutions.

Earlier, I attempted various characterizations of the individual including he who considers himself indifferent, callous to the plight of others; the types that are "naturally" virtuous and who silently practice their virtuousness; and finally, those who potentially may be good, but may not know how they can actually be good. As carefully as I am able, I should now like to consider the third case, since an overwhelming number of human beings seem to belong to this group.

There are human beings who seem to be moved to action when confronted with the suffering, mistreatment, hunger, and poverty of other human beings, even complete strangers. In spite of the strangeness of these other human beings, the potentially good are actively moved to attend to the plight of strangers. Helping others is an act by which the good express their sense of

---

[1]Agnes Heller, "The Basic Question of Moral Philosophy," *Philosophy and Social Criticism* 1 (1985): 51.

[2]Immanuel Kant, *Critique of Practical Reason* (Indianapolis: The Bobbs-Merrill Co., 1956), and Immanuel Kant, *Foundations of the Metaphysics of Morals* (Indianapolis: The Bobbs-Merrill Co., 1975).

[3]Hegel, who by stressing the role and function of institutions (constitutions, representative leaders, and participatory institutions), comes to the aid of the formal principles of morality as advanced by Kant. Ultimately Hegel complements rather than replaces Kant. See Hegel, *The Philosophy of Right* (London: Oxford University Press, 1981).

justice. Occasionally, when not confronted by the tragic dimensions of life, potentially good individuals need the supportive guidance of moral exemplars.

The potentially good's authentic effort to be and do the good and the reasonable often is hampered by forgetfulness on the one hand or lack of serious and sustained moral training in the virtues of self-control on the other. Their efforts are discouraged by the internally generated pressures of the unsocial passions which Smith described. The presence in our daily lives of these three human failings causes us to worry about the difficulty of actualizing the willingness to be good and to be just.

One difference between the exemplars and the potentially good individuals is that the exemplars are always good and often the potentially good are so only when reminded by a confrontation with suffering. Therefore, a crucial task for the potentially good is to acquire the habit of reminding themselves. Consider the following example.

A number of local papers report the famine, hunger, and homelessness in an area far away from the fairly well-to-do local community of well-meaning, law-abiding citizens. After some reflection some individuals resolve to help the unfortunate others and send money, clothing, and food. The same individuals also buy television advertisements to arouse public interest in the conditions of other people. The advertisements show pictures of starving and dying children and their devastated parents. The intent behind this effort is admirable as an implicit moral act. It is an intent propelled by conscience and by a sense of justice. The psychological effect of foreign aid and relief efforts on the starving community, however, is menacing. The donors do not see this effect.

To see the effect requires an exceptionally sensitive human being who can sense the feelings of the hungry, the unclothed, and the sick. To understand what these poor might be undergoing psychologically we must attempt intellectually and emotionally to occupy their intellectual and emotional world. Such an action is more than empathy and sympathy; it is a carefully reasoned and honestly felt emotional response, which must be guided by self-generated principles. The persons who develop self-generated principles regard themselves as potentially moral and rational human beings. They deeply reflect about their "natures," particularly about their human needs for food, shelter, and clothing. They have a basic belief in the freedom needed to secure these needs which classical moral philosophy from Plato onwards has recognized as basic to humankind's biological existence. To the extent that we are rational beings, we moderns also recognize these needs as fundamental and can ascribe them to all human beings. We can do this as rational human beings by constructing a hypothetical proposition, by a willingness to be convinced by arguments that appeal to our reasoning (cognitive) and to our moral (cognitive and emotional) capacities. By reflection, we realize that needs that are necessary for us as moral rational human beings must be necessary also for others.[4] The universality of basic human needs is readily and naturally understood by rational individuals.[5] Let us call the above conception of rationality moral rationality. It is a form that entails a capacity for reasoning and a capacity for a sense of justice propelled by what Smith called the unselfish social passions: friendliness, dutifulness, compassion, sympathy, benevolence, honesty, judiciousness, to name just a few.

There is another, narrower, concept of rationality that I would like to identify as pragmatic rationality and which the donor individuals often employ in justification of the actions of their daily lives. Individuals who act from the standpoint of pragmatic rationality do not conceive of themselves necessarily as moral. For these individuals, moral discourse does not make much sense, the term "morality" is empty, but they still consider themselves rational and pragmatic individuals. Thus, they would contend that the effects of their pragmatic rational actions are essentially the same as the effects of rational moral actions in that the effects aim at fairness and judiciousness, which are the ideals of justice broadly understood. It appears that such individuals, unlike the rational moral types, ultimately may not be resistant to the idea of reasoning from the standpoint of self-generated principles provided that these principles make practical as opposed to moral sense or that the

---

[4]Hegel, *The Philosophy of Right.*

[5]Jurgen Habermas, through the appropriation of speech acts, argues in a similar fashion. Habermas, *Theory of Communicative Action* vol. 1 (Boston: Beacon Press, 1981), 8-43.

principles are such that they have in them certain explicit advantages which may be morally questionable but are pragmatically indispensable.

There are other human needs which are not basic to existence from a biological point of view but which are necessary from the standpoint of material progress. Rational pragmatists appreciate these needs. They are needs which arose with a market economy and which in the course of time became desirable and almost as necessary as biological needs.

As is well known, the rise of science and technology brought with it the creation of hitherto unknown needs for commodities of a market economy. Markets, of course, were not born in the seventeenth century, but goods to be exchanged for money which could then result in the accumulation of capital increased in number as a result of the industrial revolution. The phenomenon is fascinating in that it continues to engage the imaginations of modernity's scientific thinkers; it is also frightening in that one witnesses the proliferation of "needs" with questionable moral relevance: hence, a throw-away paper-bag society that destroys forests. In short, the technically possible may not always be ethically acceptable, and the scientifically imaginable may not be morally acceptable.

For the first time in our Western scientific culture, distinct types of needs are rapidly becoming second nature to some human beings such as the pragmatic rational types. Once they become second nature, it becomes humanely and politically difficult to have a morally oriented discourse with those individuals who may not be able to dispense with these needs even if they are found to be morally offensive. Consider the following example. Somewhere in Africa, many hundreds of human beings are dying of hunger; some of these people have experienced self-perpetuating cycles of poverty for over three hundred years. A substantial number of scholars have carefully attempted to study the causes of the poverty in general and of hunger in particular. Their study has identified some key variables which strongly influence the continuation of poverty and hunger. They identify economic exploitation by self-centered corporations; the greed of some rich individuals; the noncaring native elites, the acceptance of economic programs which are inapplicable to the real needs of the inhabitants. These variables are carefully correlated, and the correlations suggest a relationship between poverty and hunger and the variables enumerated above. The study is widely publicized. As scientific thinkers who listen to reason, one would expect the pragmatists to be swayed by the study and challenge their government to change its policies. However, they seldom challenge their government and the question remains why. Is there a reasoning behind the resistance to the morally offensive consequences of the study from the standpoints of empirical facts, the correlation of which implicitly shows the moral bankruptcy of economic exploitation?

Pragmatic reasoning may be as follows. To live in a modern technological and industrial society is to adopt a liking for certain commodities which prescribe certain lifestyles. The liberty to freely pursue a life of happiness, private property, and access to expensive lifestyles never should be eliminated no matter how unfair the unintended consequences might be. The pragmatists might contend that individuals have the natural right of living in various lifestyles. The opponents might reply that the commodities and lifestyles might have been earned at the expense of lingering poverty and hunger for a considerable number of people elsewhere. The opponents thus attempt to change the pragmatist's actions by moral rather than rational, practical arguments.

The individuals, given their rational/pragmatic orientations, are not interested in being told that the effects of their luxurious lifestyles are morally offensive to the poor in that they contribute to their material unhappiness. When told of these effects, some people become callous and indifferent. Their opponents then shift the arguments to the pragmatic plane. They argue that if some of the poor and the hungry somehow manage to escape from the dark cave of poverty and hunger, see the bright life of material comfort and spiritual freedom, and disseminate their knowledge, the poor and the hungry are likely to explode. These poor and hungry then begin to destabilize society at the risk of being demolished by the powerful. The result of this explosion would affect the comfortable pragmatists who could lose everything, more than the poor and hungry, who have nothing to lose except their poverty. The explosion situation, if left unattended, will gradually deprive the pragmatists of the commodious life.

The pragmatists may believe that the militancy and rebellion of the poor and hungry ought to be contained by force and that there are no compelling reasons to concede too hastily. Force will contain the demands of the poor; but the exploited hungry may believe that a persistent revolve to fight for freedom despite threats and the use of force is the only road to follow. These are two seemingly irreconcilable beliefs. Between the two lies an abyss filled with the possibility of mutual destruction. But, if the pragmatists are indeed rational and pragmatic, why would they seem to accept the possibility of mutual destruction, which from all perspectives is irrational? Is this a consequence of the arrogance of power or merely shortsightedness? It may be because of both, combined with hegemonic ideas, that ridicule the transformative effect of moral arguments. The point is that we fool ourselves if we believe that possibility of revolution is distant in time and place. The French, Russian, and Chinese revolutions must indicate to us what people in despair do when suffering overwhelms joy.

The selfishness and self-centeredness of some individuals could easily become a cause of envy and hate by others. The materially poor in the continent of Africa regard the materially rich, wherever the rich reside, with resentment, envy, and hate. Resentment, envy, and hate may lead to irrational actions. Some of these actions could be that often to their own disadvantage the materially poor might sabotage the process of economic production by refusing to work even if they lose their jobs, by producing goods of inferior quality, by producing goods of unpredictable quality, or by deliberately getting fired so as to be recipients of state subsidies.

The materially poor could also organize others to engage in revolts. Revolts are tension-ridden. They feed on conditioning others to suspect and mistrust people. The mistrust can become generalized into a way of life that threatens war, which, however small, is economically expensive. The expenses of the war are collected from individual taxpayers. It is, however, unreasonable and irrational to misuse taxes for the unproductive purpose of financing war. A person's monies could be used better and more intelligently to cultivate citizens who think responsibly and autonomously to create and sustain "perpetual peace," and who believe that the creation of peace is not beyond human power. War is an irrational consequence of nonthinking combined with selfishness. Peace, on the other hand, is a reasonable condition

147

from which both the materially rich and the materially poor could benefit. Any thought which deliberately ignores the possibility of perpetual war is indirectly legitimizing irrationality as a way of life and such a way of life, economically speaking, is too costly to sustain. A rational pragmatist would be better off to desire perpetual peace than perpetual war.

So far, I have addressed the theme of thinking about justice through the guidance of principles in a general way rather than talking about Africa. There is a reason for this. The African human condition is an integral part of the human condition in general, an aspect of the universal human condition, so that the material suffering of the poor and hungry in Africa is both materially and nonmaterially interconnected with the human condition in general. The material comfort of some human beings may produce people who are incapable of empathy, of helping others. Thinking by inhabiting the place of others may lead to empathizing, or adopting certain fundamental principles which would directly enable others to take care of themselves and to found self-reliant institutions with which they can alleviate their condition of poverty, hunger, and political repression. But self-reliance cannot take place in a vacuum; it requires a consistent flow of material and nonmaterial support replete with respect, empathy, and generosity.

The ideal of self-reliance for Africa, which is the present ideal in certain theoretical writings, is empty if it is not grounded upon a realistic understanding of global political economy and Africa's place within that economy. Self-reliance can become a substantive ideal if it is combined intelligently with other strategies of development such as joint ventures and international trade. Prior to the participation within the networks of world institutions, however, certain foundational principles must be developed, principles which can be made morally, rationally, and pragmatically universal. As a beginning, Rawls' second principle must be extended and be incorporated into a genuine charter of a continental African institution, such as the Organization of African Unity, which must abolish its present abstract charters and write a truly substantive constitution.

Two principles of justice are relevant to the human condition in Africa. The first is the recognition of food, health, shelter, and clothing as inalienable human rights. African resources must be used in such a way that they can be channelled to eventually eliminate the urgent human needs of poverty and hunger, and address attendant consequences of mental and physical health, hopelessness, and undermotivation. The second principle is a demand for the duty humans may have in the recognition of freedom for those who think that they are unfree. When the basic human material needs of the African are met, then he or she may be able to think about nonmaterial human needs, such as art and religion.

The first principle demands that priority be given to enabling the poor in Africa to feed themselves. Native food producers may request the fundamental elements of food production—seeds, fertilizers, and rudimentary machinery. To supply such requests may involve the creation of a continental resource fund to which each African nation would contribute. Such a continental institution could be headed by the most capable and willing members chosen from the ranks of farmers, the primary producers, themselves. A visibility within such a continental institution may give the peasants a sense of self-respect as primary producers, a retrieval of their lost dignity. Perhaps this vision is utopian but it is better to have a utopian vision than to have no vision at all.

Some practical barriers exist which might complicate the realization of this utopian ideal. Three in particular stand out: tribalism, illiteracy, and linguistic diversity. These problems would make it difficult for the primary peasant producers to conceive of themselves as being capable of articulating their needs and aspirations in language which all Africans would understand and which would overcome the well-known problems of narrow-mindedness, clannishness, suspicions, provinciality, nationalism, will to power.[6] This cannot be solved easily.[7] The idea of a continental vision to guide examination of African problems needs as its maximum

---

[6]For an excellent analysis of the will to power, see David Booth, "Nietzche on 'The Subject as Multiplicity,'" *Man and World* 18/2 (1985): 121-47.

[7]For a perceptive discussion of the theme that African philosophy needs to conceive of itself as a pragmatically oriented solver of human problems, see Lansana Keita, "Contemporary African Philosophy: the Search for a Method," *Praxis International* 5/2 (July 1985): 145-62.

requirement the availability of Africans able to generate principles which demand that they be citizens of a continent rather than merely parts of families, tribes, groups, and nations at war with one another. Poverty, hunger, and war are widespread problems, continentally shared in Africa and deeply affected by the legacies of Arab slavery and European colonialism in the past, and the mismanagement of African and non-African hegemonic elites in the present.

The first principle requires the helping hands of science and technology to encourage the efforts of African peasants to feed and clothe themselves using indigenous technologies to learn Western high technology. The result may be a synthesis, a contribution from African soil to the human heritage, and the proper use of African internal resources for global usage. A result would be a retrieval of identity, dignity, and pride for the peasants themselves.

The poor would thus begin to look at themselves not merely as recipients of charity and foreign aid but as innovators of models of self-development, working with the help of the science and technology provided by the Western world.

Africa's Material Resources

We now want to examine the kind of human and material resources which exist in Africa and the actions which the African poor on the one hand and the African elites and leaders on the other hand must undertake if Africa is to develop through the power of self-reliant institutions.

Discussion of material resources is necessary so that principles may be founded upon them. Principles are empty if they are not grounded upon material resources, and development of material resources is blind if unguided by principles. It is principles that give human beings visions of themselves, their essential human powers to transform the world to conform with their ideas. The continent of Africa is blessed with material resources but these resources are neither systematically interpenetrated with policies guided by self-generated principles nor developed by sophisticated science and technology.[8] African resources are dormant, occupying space. This space ought to be energized by an appropriate theory of development.

The basic requirement of such a theory is a scientific, technological transformation. If hunger, poverty, political repression, and war were not part of the contemporary human condition in Africa, then Africans could leave undisturbed nature and its material resources in Africa; nature as in precolonial Africa could be treated as the endless stream of humankind's aesthetic joy. Nature itself could be viewed aesthetically, a focus of moral sensibilities.[9] But the contemporary Africans cannot view nature reverently and aesthetically because poverty, hunger, political repression, and wars are perennial features of their everyday lives. These discomforts can be removed only if nature is explored by morally sensitive science and technology. In the process of this scientific and technological exploration, however, maximum moral attention must be given to the silent rights of nature. The scientific and technological transformation must be done with great caution lest Africa reproduce the detrimental conditions in parts of the Western world where science and technology have produced the possibility of ending human life on the planet. If Africa is to survive in the modern world, it must master the nuances of the scientific attitude in an ethically motivated manner if it is to benefit all of humankind.

The goals of Africa are many but three stand out. First, African material resources must be carefully assessed and an ethical form of technology and science found for them. Second, Africa as a whole must strive for scientific and technological independence from industrial countries and develop self-reliant institutions which would be able to survive in an already interdependent world and

---

[8]For a detailed discussion of science and technology and their relevance for Africa's future, see Isebill V. Gruhn, "Towards Scientific and Technological Independence," *The Journal of Modern African Studies* 22/1 (1984): 1-19.

[9]For development of this theme, see Tedros Kiros, "Alienation and Aesthetics in Marx and Tolstoy: A Comparative Analysis," *Man and World* 18/8 (1985): 171-85.

which could take the form of a new world order. Third, African developers must pay maximum attention to training African nationals "to develop a science based peasant agriculture." In the words of Uma Lele,

> Between 80 and 90 percent of the nearly 400 million people in sub-Saharan Africa live in rural areas. Most derive their subsistence from meager crop and live stock production and survive on annual per capita incomes of less than U.S. $150. Although production is geared largely to subsistence, the rural sector is also the major source of food for urban consumption and of raw materials for exports and domestic manufacturing. Except in a few mineral-producing countries, such as Zaire, Zambia, and Nigeria, agriculture constitutes the largest income-generating sector, contributing up to 40 percent of the gross national product of many African countries.[10]

The short-run goal of Africa then ought to be a carefully thought out scheme for enabling Africans to become completely capable of feeding themselves, as they were doing about 1957. The fundamental need in Africa as a whole is the conquest of famine. Uma Lele was right when he proposed that food self-sufficiency is superior to the commercialization and industrialization of agriculture.

Human needs in Africa are both technical and ethical. The technical questions need a detailed mastery of African material resources if they are to be answered. I have already described all human beings as potentially capable of thinking about justice through self-generated principles, and have suggested that moral/rational and the rational/pragmatic humans would help Africans develop self-reliant institutions within the context of the world market by means of international trade and joint ventures. These strategies are of course limited to the technology, but indigenous

---

[10]Uma Lele, "Rural Africa: Modernization, Equity, and Long-term Development," in *A Technical Memorandum Congress of the United States*, December, 1984, p. 98. See also Sarah B. Berry, *Fathers Work for Their Sons* (Berkeley: University of California Press, 1985).

African developers, particularly the technocrats, need to be cautious not to be limited by technology to the detriment of the moral rational dimension—the dimension of thinking under the guidance of self-generated principles. Thus, the urgent material human needs may only be met if every technical strategy is penetrated by moral sentiments, the social passions in particular. Unless the technical is interpenetrated by the moral/ethical, the human condition in Africa might not be "solved" in a way which is acceptable to African capitalists, city elites, and the poor. The ideal of course is the combination of food self-sufficiency through small scale farms on the one hand, and large scale commercial farms on the other. If these two goals cannot be met simultaneously, then it makes sense for food self-sufficiency to be given priority over the commercialization and industrialization of agriculture. Hungry African labor cannot be expected to perform efficiently.

The minimum requirement for self-generated principles of the African poor and elite is the availability of a reasonable amount of material resources. The current food crises in more than twenty-two African countries and the startling nonexistence of nutritional resources give no signs that the problems will be adequately overcome. There prevail signs of hope, however, in some of the well-reasoned analysis of Africa's material resources which project a better future. Irving Markovitz, the well-known student of Africa's political economy, paraphrasing Patel, has written a passage which deserves to be quoted in full:

> Surendra Patel, in another forward-looking analysis, emphasizes the enormous potential of the continent. The amount of arable land in Africa is more than twice that of Latin America or China. It is nearly one and a half times that of India, and Africa has only half of India's population and a climate ideally suited to growing all kinds of crops both for human consumption and for industrial raw materials. The land that is usable for grazing of cattle, the unlimited opportunities for fishing, and rich forest resources await tapping. Although the continent already produces nearly one seventh of the world's minerals, almost every day brings major new discoveries. The Sahara, for example,

has turned out to be dry of water but rich in oil. With oil and gas in the north, coal in the South, and hydropower in the center, with Africa's mighty rivers accounting for 40% of the world's potential hydroelectric power, the continent's energy potential appears unlimited. Nevertheless, with 8 percent of the world population, the continent can boast of only 2 percent of world production, less than half of the United Kingdom.[11]

Some people may think that the optimism of a thinker such as Markovitz, who is known for his "radical" inclinations, may sound much more convincing if compared with Carl Eicher, who has a somewhat different political persuasion. Eicher has written as follows:

Africa's food and poverty problems should not be allowed to overshadow some impressive achievements of the continent over the past twenty-five years. Foremost is the increase in average life-expectancy from an estimated thirty-eight years in 1950 to almost fifty years in 1980. This 30 percent increase is often overlooked by those who are mesmerized by rates of economic growth. Moreover, the achievements in education have been impressive in some countries, and there has been a vast improvement in the capacity of countries such as Nigeria, Kenya, the Ivory Coast, Cameroon, and Malawi to organize, plan, and manage their economies.[12]

The passage from Markovitz directly equips us with concrete data which reinforce the need for overcoming the fundamental problem of necessity which is particularly devastating in the African context. Material necessity can be overcome primarily by the

---

[11]Irving Leonard Markovitz, *Power and Class in Africa* (Prentice Hall, 1977), p. 329.

[12]See Lele, "Rural Africa," 103-8, and see the first chapter reference to Michael Lipton's work in this book.

forces of oil, coal, and hydropower. Africa is not destitute of potential energy, of human power, and of formally educated people. With all the necessary material and human resources, why are the problems of poverty, hunger, and political repression still characteristic of the contemporary human condition in Africa? The answer is to be found in the nature of the people who might otherwise bring about change: self-interested politicians, elites, and classes, urban-biased developers, poorly trained native and foreign nationals, and unsophisticated administrators. Furthermore, there exists a critical lack of basic education. Material resources have not been used always to satisfy the needs of the African poor, the peasants, and the wage laborers. The needs of the rich Africans are not the same as the needs of the very poor Africans. A need for late model cars which typically politicians and elites purchase, is not of the same intensity to the landless and poor peasants as is the need for fertilizers, durable tractors, and seeds. The first type of need is highly specialized and well beyond the struggle for food, clothing, and shelter.

African material resources clearly have been abused in the hands of the perpetuators of hegemonic ideas: inept politicians, urban elites, home grown and foreign-trained officials, and expatriate planning advisers.[13] The primary causes of the abuse of African material resources are mismanagement and the inappropriate transfer of technology. These contribute not to the improvement of Africa's future but to the dangerous possibility of neocolonialism. Nigeria, Kenya, the Ivory Coast, Cameroon, and Malawi are qualified exceptions. One possible way of preventing the danger of neocolonialism is the continental approach to the study and resolution of the human condition in Africa. The idea of a continental approach is a concrete example of a counter-hegemonic vision.

It is Africans themselves who should attend to the needs of the poorest Africans. It is no longer justified or relevant to blame outside powers for originating poverty and hunger in Africa. What is needed is that Africans themselves, by means of reason combined with imagination and moral powers, innovate technologies, and

---

[13]For an extensive bibliography that discusses these issues and many others, see *Africa Tomorrow: Issues in Technology, Agriculture, and U.S. Foreign Aid* of December 1984.

sciences, face hunger and poverty guided by the internalization of the first principle. The first principle has a sufficient number of substantive ideas that can lead to the eventual development of effective policies with continental and global visions. The rest is a matter of application.

When the basic human needs of the poor are met, as articulated by the first principle, it makes sense that the spiritually profound needs articulated in the second principle receive attention. These are the needs for freedom, art, and religion. Freedom as a goal should work very closely with revitalizing the hitherto repressed moral sentiments as described by Smith. In this way Africans would be able to develop self-reliant institutions within Africa to translate the imperatives of the first principle into actualities that work. In this way, the theoretical premise of the first principle is given concrete form—the form of freedom grounded upon self-reliant institutions. Theory is converted into practice. Thus, absolutely binding principles such as the first two principles may enable the rationally pragmatic and moral citizens of the materially developed world to help those Africans who are willing to help themselves. These proposals, however, need to be carefully explicated and concertized.

Moral Philosophy and Africa's Political Economy

> How can a philosophy relate to a culture? There seem to be just four possibilities: (1) it can express the culture, (2) it can affect it, (3) it can both express it and affect it, so that there is interaction between them, or (4) it can be independent of it. And it seems clear it can do any of the four in more or less degree.
>
> Marus G. Singer

> I think then that the chief task of philosophy is to justify this way of reason against the domination of technology based on science. That is the point of philosophic hermeneutic. It corrects the peculiar falsehood of modern consciousness: the idolatry of scientific method and the anonymous authority of the sciences and it vindicates against the noblest task of the citizen—decision making

according to one's responsibility—instead of conceding that task to the expert. . .

Gadamer

Technology is not the mastery of nature, but of the relation between nature and humanity.

Walter Benjamin

In the passages quoted above, Singer in particular attempts to preserve a definite place for philosophy in its age-old function of guiding humans to live the life of reflection, meditation, and deliberation—a life guided by the wish to think for, evaluate, and judge ourselves and be judged by others. If and when the human freely introduces thinking or philosophizing as such to become one of its dominant values or norms,[14] and thus willingly engages in letting thinking or philosophizing be its chief guide in the daily activities of choosing, judging, deciding, evaluating, and deliberating activities that occupy our everyday lives, then the human will have embraced philosophy as a dimension of its self-created culture. In this extended sense, philosophy itself becomes a culture by effecting and expressing a particular way of life—a way of being human.

Not everyone may choose to live this particular way of life. Certainly the exemplary moral persons will find it conceptionally welcome. Indeed, their exemplary view of themselves and that of others is guided by thinking and philosophizing in such a way that they live philosophy; they no longer need to be converted to accept thinking and philosophizing to guide their lives. Their lives already have become affected and their philosophy is concretely expressed in actions which are guided consistently by self-generated principles. Their exemplary actions are written in the exemplar's willingness to follow the path of justice. Such

---

[14] This definition of a norm was formulated by Adrian M. S. Piper in "Two Conceptions of the Self," *Journal of Philosophy* 18/2 (Sept. 1985): 173-99. By a norm is meant "a recommendation, principle, rule, or law that prescribes behavior in the service of some favored goal; call such behavior purposive" (182).

individuals know how and what to do when they choose, evaluate, and judge. Applying this reasoning to Africa, we can say that such individuals do not look at themselves merely as members of a nation, a region, a class, or a professional circle, but consider themselves primarily as human beings who were born in the African continent. As the members of both a fortunate continent because of its rich material resources, and an unfortunate continent because of the suffering of an overwhelming majority of the population, they bear the burdens of the human condition in Africa.

Certainly such ideal types are not readily available in Africa. Perhaps not even one exists in the continent. The possible non-existence of exemplary individuals in Africa, however, does not mean that such human types cannot come into being. The problem of the possibility of their nonexistence then is not so much a problem of the impossibility of nurturing such individuals as it is a problem of unwillingness to envision such a person. If people are willing to envision such exemplars and agree that they would be good for Africa, then there remains the task of nurturing such pan-African citizens.

African educators are advised to reeducate themselves in order to educate the African generation of students to be responsible citizens for whom thinking or philosophizing under the guidance of self-generated principles would become the norm. This goal of African education is one of the major tasks upon which African educators and policy setters should embark. Thinking through self-generated moral principles will develop individuals in Africa capable of looking at themselves as moral/rational human beings who have the capacity to think for and to inhabit the horizons of others. This possible way of my looking at the human condition in Africa is the continental perspective. The time has come in Africa for Africans to critically reevaluate their tendency to look at themselves merely as family, tribe, village, group, or nation fighting among themselves. There may be wars for self-determination that are worth fighting; perhaps the time has come, however, when the quest for self determination could be solved by negotiations among Africans themselves. Negotiations and principled discussions are not the dreams of idealists. During times of crisis, negotiations and discussions would contribute more to solving Africa's immediate needs for food, shelter, and clothing than expensive wars that reflect the domestic policies of rich and materially developed nations. These nations should give their immediate attention to wars for self-determination in Africa as should African educators and policy makers. Self-determination, poverty, and hunger should be examined from a continental perspective.

One way of enabling human beings to think for others is through the generation of principles. Once these self-generated principles are specified and adopted, then it would be a matter of time for these principles to provide a moral vision of humankind. After disciplined struggles, if these principles in our daily lives are joyous, fulfilling, and pleasure-giving rather than painful, then it would be relatively easy for individuals to freely habituate themselves to life guided by self-generated principles.

In a highly abstract sense, discussions of self-generated principles deal more with a form of thinking than they do with the content of thinking. On this level, our concern has been with the human being as such wherever that individual actually lives. Any human may be capable of thinking and acting from the standpoint of self-generated principles. Rawls formulated the idea of the veil of ignorance as a hypothetical device which would enable individuals to dissociate themselves from the stronghold which tradition, common sense, culture, and religion have on their daily lives such that it becomes extremely difficult to adopt principles that are free from tradition, common sense, culture, and religion. Rawls envisioned that the veil of ignorance would enlighten individuals with that which does not easily and naturally come to them. In this abstract way, Rawls has also dealt with the form of thinking, but he does not leave the matter there. He also attempts to specify the content of principles. These principles are ones which he abstracts not from the human self outside of history, such as Descartes' famous third meditation of the meditations, but from the history of an industrial technological society.

The central principles which dominate the value system of such a society are the principles of liberty and wealth. These principles are not eternal principles that define humanity's ideal goods. These principles for example were severely criticized by Plato throughout the *Republic*, but particularly in the context of his discussion of the human desires, especially the appetitive desires, which resist control by reason in the human soul.[15] The kinds of principles then that one might generate among other things are affected by education, indoctrination, and alienation which are dominant in a given time, place, and culture. The possibility of an appropriate human environment which respects the life of reflection and the possible consequence of knowledge informing everyday life under the guidance of self-generated principles may become an ideal for human beings. The particular principles themselves, however, may never become eternal so that present and future generations will freely internalize them. Rawls stressed insufficiently the sense in which the conceptions of justice may be regulative ideals, but that their particular contents are at best colored by dominant values to which the members of an industrial technological society have become socialized. The hegemonic power of such socialization raises the question, Did these individuals generate these principles or did they absorb them as they found them in the form of tradition?

Within the framework of the concerns of an industrial technological society, the principles of justice which Rawls has formed have become almost second nature; they have resulted in the manifestation of deep inequalities which contaminate the ideas of justice. For Rawls, the question of the genealogy of these principles is not as important as the fact that these principles are not equally accessible to all citizens, and that they ought to be, given that individuals have become so socialized that they view these principles as indispensable and necessary. Rawls' formulation of thinking is right from the standpoint of principles when individuals decide to view themselves as rational and moral selves. However his two principles of justice which apply to the needs of a modern industrial technological society must be revised when discussing the human condition in Africa.

The second principle of justice, which was formulated to handle the problem of deep inequalities in the political, social, and economic spheres obtaining in democratic regimes, ought to be extended to apply to the human condition in Africa, to the issues

---

[15]For a careful discussion of the human desires as such, see the relevant passages in books 4, 6, 7, and 9, where the tyranny of appetitive needs is discussed. *The Republic of Plato*, trans. and ed. Allan Bloom (New York: Basic Books, 1968).

of poverty, hunger, political repression, and war. Put differently, the internal problems of Africa can be articulated in a carefully reasoned way such that the various rational/moral and moral/pragmatic human types in democratic regimes can be convinced that they have an obligation to help others so that the others can help themselves. African internal problems are so universal that they can activate the moral sentiments of humankind. The aspirations and desires of rich African elites are by no means representative of the real needs of the peasants who form the overwhelming majority of Africans.[16] The poorest sections of this peasantry have yet to guarantee themselves food, clothing, and shelter. The needs of food, shelter, and clothing are so fundamental that they define our human nature. As argued in chapter 1, the need for food is an inalienable human need; therefore food should be made readily available to all human beings. For those who are in the position to help others, poverty and hunger in Africa kindle moral sentiments, particularly the social ones of generosity, humanity, kindness, and compassion. The Kantian view of the self as morally dutiful is applicable here.

There is an absolute need for food, clothing, and minimally acceptable housing in Africa. To satisfy these needs we must formulate some principles of justice. Chapter 5 showed the reasons (moral, rational, and pragmatic) which may enable people outside of Africa to view African problems as their own. Such individuals may convert their moral sentiments into practical projects in the form of technological assistance such as agricultural machinery or oxen. Intelligent use of agricultural machinery purchased at a reasonable price is one of the practicable ways with which the first principle of justice can receive an institutional structure.[17]

Continental Thinking and Principles

The rational pragmatic types in contemporary Africa need to undergo a fundamental transformation if they are to play an

---

[16]The theme has been argued forcefully by Franz Fanon in *The Wretched of the Earth* (New York: Grove Press, 1967), 148-206.

[17]See Habermas, *Theory*, 60-61.

effective role in contributing to the material development of Africa. Among other things, African intellectual elites should become selfless, un-self-centered, and willing to think about tribal, national, and regional problems in continental terms. They must view themselves as Africans, as responsible members of the whole continent, rather than nationals of particular countries. A continental state of mind is needed in the analysis of tribal, national, and regional African problems. They are problems of all of Africa, and a continental approach must be employed in the attempt at solving them. The nations in Africa ought to view themselves as members of a continent challenged by fundamental continentwide problems.

We might as well assume that the human in general is in bondage, and each human individual is really not complete. What is needed to complete our humanity is commitment to norms such as peace, justice, and freedom. These norms are so sublime that the individual, upon incorporating them into its very being, may one day enjoy their positive effects by living in an ethical community, a community that is run by self-generated principles. Such a community is worth dreaming about; it may be a dream with real substance, real promises, and an alternative perhaps for both the Hobbesian and the modern deconstructionist as a will to power, when the will to power is negatively understood. The possibility of the founding of a human community with new moral ideals may after all be an alternative to the closed world of self-seeking competitive individuals of some circles of the postmodern deconstructionist tradition.[18]

African and Global Ethical Communities

Thinking and reflection should precede the adoption of specific principles. Pragmatists in particular should ask themselves whether they are convinced that principles are worth having. Would they be guided by these self-generated principles and abandon the tempting dispositions of their other human impulses? They must sacrifice some of their commodious lifestyles in order to achieve alternative economic arrangements in a community.

---

[18]For a searching critique of deconstruction, see Richard Eldridge, "Deconstruction and Its Alternatives," *Man and World* 18/2 (1985): 121-47.

They must also be willing to engage in Smith's moral sentiments for the betterment of all those others whom they cannot see or touch directly. To act from the standpoint of principles is to forego wasteful luxuries as morally and rationally inappropriate.

Rawls has argued that people who may wish to live by rational principles do not have to view themselves as moral beings. It is enough for some people to have a political as opposed to a metaphysical conception of justice. The rationally pragmatic may find Rawls' argument particularly appealing. He wrote as follows:

> One thing I failed to say in *A Theory of Justice*, or failed to stress sufficiently is that justice as fairness is intended as a political conception of justice. While a political conception of justice is, of course, a moral conception, it is a moral conception worked out for a specific kind of subject, namely for political, social, and economic institutions. In particular, justice as fairness is framed to apply to what I have called the "basic structure" of a modern constitutional democracy. By this structure, I mean such a society's main political, social, and economic institutions, and how they fit together into one unified system of social cooperation for different kinds of societies existing under different historical and social conditions, or whether it can be extended to a general moral conception, or a significant part thereof, are altogether separate questions.[19]

There are certain lessons to be drawn from the above discussion which pragmatic thinkers can use to justify their desires to help Africans help themselves:

1. African peasants' and workers' efforts to improve their productivity require the strengthening of science and technology

---

[19]Rawls has apparently revised the fundamental thesis of his *A Theory of Justice* with respect to his conception of the human self. See John Rawls, "Justice or Fairness: Political or Metaphysical," *Philosophy an Public Affairs* 14/3 (1985).

163

2.   Most of the science and technology, including research and planning, is in the hands of Western and some Eastern nations. The pragmatists are the possessors of some of the scientific and technical knowledge

3.   African peasants and workers have been systematically denied first-hand scientific and technical knowledge

4.   African peasants and workers wish to strengthen their science and technology. The pragmatists who possess the scientific and technical knowledge are advised to work with them (Table 1)

5.   It is economically irrational and politically unwise for the pragmatic producers of profit that indirectly contribute to the overexploitation of the African peasants and workers to sell them technical/scientific knowledge. Peasants and workers are unemployed, or are employed but do not have enough private capital, or have some capital but the technological/scientific knowledge they wish to buy is too costly

6.   The high cost of technological/scientific knowledge may lead to the disappearance of a market

7.   The disappearance of a market may lead to the reduction of the standards of living for relevant individuals in the Western world

There could be political repercussions of unreasonable profit margins which would have serious economic implications as well. One of these is that the unemployed, underemployed, homeless, and poverty-stricken may revolt against the West and wreck African resources, part of which go into the making of scientific and technological commodities in the West. Such destruction would have a direct impact on the Western productive system itself. Furthermore, in Africa a nonproductive and a revolutionary unemployed class without any purchasing power destroys a potentially viable market. The market turns into a sanctuary of agitated, resentful, alienated Africans determined to destroy the wealth of humankind. It is potentially dangerous to neglect the intelligence of Africans by unreasonable and shortsighted attitudes. It is both economically and politically wise to empower Africans economically so that they can participate in the world economic system as productive and autonomous economic and political subjects. Such a rational decision may eventually produce both a self-reliant African community and an ethical world community

Table 1

TAXONOMY OF POTENTIAL MEASURES FOR STRENGTHENING AFRICAN SCIENCE AND TECHNOLOGY CAPABILITIES[20]

Group I:	Measures to Develop Scientific and Technological Infrastructure and Institutions
A.	Establish or expand national, regional, or local research institutions, and create the necessary network for them in key economic sectors.
B.	Develop science-planning bodies, academies of science, and research councils.
C.	Establish funding mechanisms for private research.
D.	Train research managers and administrators.
Group II:	Measures to Develop Science and Technology Support Services
A.	Train technical staff for science laboratories.
B.	Establish facilities for the maintenance and repair of equipment.
C.	Establish technical norms and standards.

---

[20]For a concrete model that heavily draws from the Ethiopian experience with many suggestions which, by extension, apply to the African experience of struggling to overcome material underdevelopment, see Keith Griffin and Roger Hay, "Problems of Agricultural Development in Socialist Ethiopia: An Overview and a Suggested Survey," *The Journal of Peasant Studies*, 13/1 (Oct. 1985): 37-67. Particularly impressive is their view that out of the multiplicity of modes of production that are extant in modern Ethiopia—peasant farms, service cooperatives, state farms, and pastoral farms—the service cooperative is superior in terms of efficiency and potential equity. The key component in the service cooperative is the notion of cooperation oriented toward development. This idea holds the key to the material development of Africa.

Table 1 (continued)

D. Develop information systems, including libraries and museums.

E. Institute geodesical and geographical surveys, meteorological services, and the like.

F. Develop national and regional consulting services.

Group III: Development of Education

A. Develop graduate and undergraduate science and technology programs.

B. Improve secondary and primary school science education.

C. Develop technical training schools and apprenticeship schemes.

D. Strengthen manpower analysis and forecasting.

E. Increase adult literacy.

Group IV: Measures to Improve International Scientific Exchange

A. Organize national, regional, and international research networks.

B. Encourage travel, conferences, and the exchange of information and scientists.

C. Take measures to control the brain drain.

6

THE MORAL PHILOSOPHY OF DEVELOPMENT

Chapter 1 mentioned that to a considerable extent the food crisis in Africa is man-made. The African continent, particularly the eastern part, has had famines for many years. Famines and food crises are part of the diachronic structure of African history, one of the dimensions of the tragic life in Africa.

Africa today has inherited in a depressing manner sacrosanct and backward modes of food production. The continent as a whole is intellectually, emotionally, and culturally dependent on hegemonic ideas imported from Europe and North America.

Europe can look to its great philosophers, America to its technological innovations, particularly in space exploration and medical science, and Asia to its economic miracles. Africa has nothing to glorify. It has only hunger, famine, disease, corruption, blind pride, turbulence, national wars, and economic disasters. To think of Africa, for many people, is to think of "darkness," sadness, and hopelessness amid gigantic natural resources.

Africa has resources, gold and diamonds in the southern tip, cotton, coffee, sugar, in the western and eastern regions. The minds and hearts which should develop the resources have imprisoned themselves in hegemonic political and economic ideas which enrich a few urban dwellers and privileged peasants. The majority of Africans, primarily the poor peasants, are languishing without hope, work, or prospects. The children are too under-nourished, too emotionally and culturally impoverished to serve as a backbone for any continental transformation.

The state of children's minds and bodies is a sign of a nation's future. For Africa the future is bleak, almost nonexistent. Without an intellectually active, literate population, the continent cannot be developed. African power holders seem blind to the shocking facts that surround them every day. They have become sleepwalkers. They have become intoxicated by hegemonic ideas that literally kill imaginative and reflective thought. The hegemonic power of ideas accounts for the depressing condition of contemporary African everyday life. African children are being born to a continent without food, without housing, and without clothing. The eyes of African children are reminders of the dehumanization and destruction of the self. A self which is not fed cannot think, plan, or imagine. Such a soulless self cannot participate in the demanding project of modernization with a moral vision.

The food crisis in Africa is not merely a failure perpetuated by greedy, inept, and good-for-nothing African leaders. It also is a manifestation of a moral crisis with a global scope. The failure of poor African peasants to feed themselves is caused partly because people outside Africa greedily, callously, and maliciously accumulate commodities that they do not need. The privileged ones have internalized the vices manufactured by capital: profit, indifference, cruelty, one-sidedness, and amoral and calculative reason. These subtle vices which afflict the soul are the sources of the hegemonic ideas which kill dreams, frustrate hopes, depress the psyche, cripple the imagination, and empty vision. Human beings have reached the point at which they can no longer look at food as an inalienable right of the hungry, but rather as a commodity, a good, a thing for sale. Those human beings who do not have the money with which to buy food are condemned to die.

The food crisis in Africa is literally manufactured by the failures of intelligence, moral responsibility, and reason. It is caused by the hegemonic vices of the African and non-African owners of the means of production. Holders of power have internalized the vices of capital and have become enslaved to money, status, symbolic power, arrogance, and vanity.

What a person becomes or fails to become is deeply affected by that person's conception of self. If a person thinks that selfishness, greed, and envy are intrinsically bad, he or she will act contrary to them and develop a sense of self that is contrary to the vices so consistently abhorred.

When Africans and Europeans encountered each other for the first time, their conceptions of the self were radically different. The differences, however, were not those of psychic structures.

Their differences were reflections of socialization and enculturation to hegemonic ideas which were adopted to the point that they seemed to be integral aspects of the psyche. Hegemonic ideas, however, need not be adopted psychically to be a compelling force in human behavior. It is enough if people believe in them.

The differences between the African and the European may be characterized as follows. For the most part, the African peasant's conception of nature was essentially unaggressive, mystical, and fearful. The peasant seemed to prefer subordinating himself or herself to nature rather than to pursuing it aggressively to submission and transformation. Material development requires a view of nature as inferior to man's prowess and intelligence. For development, it is crucial that nature yield to man. The soft, respectful, and intimidated attitude of the African peasant was antithetical to the conditions needed to conquer nature.

The European conception of nature was that of mastery, confrontation, and transformation. Whereas the African peasant bowed to nature, the European exploiter of its minerals and rich soil attacked it; while the African peasant was overwhelmed by nature's sublimity, the European raped it; while the African peasant refused to cut the trees and clear the land, the European could do it with massive tractors in a few hours. These outlooks toward nature are markedly different as are the consequences for development.

The two different attitudes toward nature also are manifest in the moral and practical dimension of the first encounter of the African and the European. The European explorer came to Africa in search of wealth. He found the continent of Africa a concrete land of resources which became the basis of material development. His African brethren were "invented," to use Mudimbe's phrase, as "others" who stood in the explorer's way. If the project of development, the development of Europe, necessitated it the "primitive," "good-natured," "force-worshipping" other would be eliminated. The systematic, albeit short, colonization of the other was an act of taming and the eventual destruction of the identity of the "other" in Africa. When development required it, the other's "humanity" was sacrificed to the fortunes and resources of the continent of Africa. The African peasant was surprised when the explorer arrived.

The African conception of morality displayed itself in the generosity of the African peasants' acceptance of the European explorer. The African looked at the European as a brother whose intentions were not evil. The African peasant must have used his own soul as a measure to judge the soul of the other. The first encounter then was not between good and evil. It was characterized by anxiety, curiosity, suspicion, wonder, and a sense of love for the stranger. The African peasant was fascinated by the Europeans. He was disposed toward living with the other, however strange the other looked, behaved, and thought. There was a degree of living and letting live. It was in seeking to understand and control the temptation to judge the Europeans that the African conception of development began to unfold.

The African peasant was willing to understand the European explorer without judgment. The European on the other hand came to the continent armed with the language of judgment. He ridiculed a mind and heart that refused to cut trees and to attack nature as intrinsically primitive and backward, ready to be subjected to hegemonic ideas such as religion, science, and political economy. The European explorer's language of judgment had a genealogy of ideas that the European fused with his very being, his cerebral and moral fiber. The hegemonic ideas were firmly imprinted upon his character, his language, and his disrespectful attitude toward the African peasant. For the European, the African peasant was indispensable for development. As an other, the peasant was a commodity and a source of unpaid labor.

The African peasant was not fully conscious that the European did not recognize his humanity. As a consequence, the African did not morally and technologically prepare himself to defend his dignity against colonialism. With his passive view of nature, he did not master technology. The African peasant's conception of morality vacillated. A vacillating person reflects too much to fight a colonialism which fed on cruelty and a perverse sense of hate propelled by pseudocourage. Moral fortitude, the disposition of the African peasant, was precisely what was not needed during the encounter.

The power of the European to abuse and exploit Africans resulted in the killing of his conscience, his inner reason. Because of the death of inner reason, the European could confront the inverted other and use him for his own ends. It was the presence of conscience, of inner reason in the African peasant's soul, that prevented him from (a) destroying external nature in order to produce technology, therefore setting the stage for development; (b) using the militaristic aspect of technology against the European colonizer; and (c) developing a conception of morality that dehumanizes the other, so that it can without any remorse use the other as a thing, a means, and not as an intrinsically noble end which commands respect.

Chapter 2 argued these ideas by drawing together the positive insights of the various schools of thought which have thought through the question of African underdevelopment. Added to these is the insight that the African peasant's conception of morality and development has contributed to underdevelopment and hunger in Africa. The current food crisis in African is rooted in the African peasant's and European colonizer's radically different conceptions of morality, external nature, and each other's humanity. In order to understand the present, we must look at that original encounter from the aspect of the hegemonic power of ideas. Historians have done a remarkable job of documenting the brutalities of slavery and colonialism as acts of violence. They have done relatively little concerning the ideas which shaped the violent colonizer and his victims. Ideas can be more brutal than guns. The hand that shot the bullet from the gun of the colonizer was directed by a hidden thought which legitimized the killing of the other. Ideas are as crucial as force since humans are both spiritual and material.

Africa has much to offer itself and the world. It is a continent of hope. Hope could be illusory if it is not backed up by tough thoughts. Africa is a continent which is testing the will, stamina, and imagination of its proud, religious, and industrious peasants. They are transforming African agriculture. There are signs of hope in Zimbabwe, Kenya, Uganda, and Nigeria. Of course, a liberated South Africa would provide a wave of modernization under the guidance of compassionate blacks and whites.

Chapter 3 and the remainder of the book construct a theory of development which is appropriate to the human condition in Africa. The theory draws from two bodies of thought: Western political economy and moral philosophy, particularly Adam Smith and the contemporary political philosopher John Rawls; and

171

African philosophy buttressed by the African peasants' ordinary moral and social practices in the context of Husserl's conceptions of the life-world.

The contemporary readers of Adam Smith have read him as an economist who either neglected morality or developed a morality that legitimizes the selfish and greedy passions. In fact, Smith understood the limits of the capitalist market when it callously neglected the role of morality. His subtle understanding of human nature suggested that unless the selfish and unsocial passions were regulated by the social and compassionate ones, the capitalist market itself would not endure. The excess of the selfish passions, Smith argued, could destroy the quest for profit and the maximization of utility. There is a reasonable and unreasonable way of running the market. A market that is systematically denuded of the the moral dimension cannot deliver luxury commodities constantly and safely. Insofar as a person has purchasing power, any commodity is obtainable. Consumers know this. What they are unwilling to know is that in Africa each time person A accumulates commodity B, person C is correspondingly sinking into poverty. There is an indirect relationship between wealth and poverty in Africa. The defense of the rich man of his wealth in statements such as "I worked hard for it" does not disguise the invisible process of the extraction of surplus value from the concrete labor of modern African laborers. Marx taught us the systematic process of the exploitation of labor.

Whatever one's opinion of Marx, he forces us to see holes in classical political economy, in its view of the exploitation of man by man as natural or nonexistent. Marx exploded the prejudices of classical political economy beyond any hope of restoration.

When one is armed with the morally powerful insights of Smith, particularly his recommendation to economists not to violate the silent cries of human moral sentiments, one is bound to look at the human condition in Africa as the arena in which care, compassion, love, and cooperation are invisible. There one finds no extension of Smith's moral sentiments to the African, particularly to the poor and illiterate African peasants and the displaced *lumpenproletariat* of African cities.

If human beings were to attain their full common sense as well as their tough intelligence, the moral sentiments which Smith articulated could be reconstructed in a way that could energize the

African peasants and create an economic order as yet unwitnessed in Africa. Human beings are full of surprises. African peasants are no exception. They have been waiting for years to be consulted about the condition of their land, their oxen, and the fertilizers that they want. Yet the Western scientists have ridiculed the rich practical knowledge of the peasant. The expert wants to displace the peasant's hard-won experience. The peasant on the other hand resists modernization. The expert wants the peasant to take inconsequential courses from ill-prepared high school students. The peasant heaps abuse on the young teachers and threatens to shoot them.

One way of understanding the relationships between the expert, the symbol of modernization, and the peasant, the symbol of tradition and custom, is to consider it in terms of Husserl's life-world and modernity. The African peasants are reflective, custom-abiding, and superstitious. They are guided by practical wisdom as Aristotle understood the term. They are not merely identityless parts of a group, as Temples regarded the Bantu peasants. Rather they are rugged individuals conscious of their social practices, myths, and language games. They are convinced that they have a culture to defend, traditions to uphold, myths to embrace, ways of plowing land, and medicines which invigorate their souls. In the presence of the expert, the peasants are committed to the prescientific life-world which has housed them comfortably for centuries. That they are conservative, suspicious, and resistant to change should not make them impenetrable others.

For Husserl the life-world is prescientific. It is a pregiven world accompanied by myths, superstitions, dogmatic beliefs. The life-world is the world of religion, and allows the appropriation of natural resources by physical labor. It is not a world of mathematical formulas, theorems, laws, axioms, and technological tools. In the life-world, as in the African precolonial world, knowledge is intuitive and not analytic. Things are intuitively knowable, particularly if one is favored by the gods. The poor and the hungry are not favored by the gods so that, following traditional belief, their plight cannot be overcome by analytic programs. Within the life-world of African peasants, major human catastrophes such as famines belong to the mystical, hidden and unknowable, prescientific order of things.

173

Any mind that is passionately convinced that there is a preexisting, rigid and right way of ordering the world deserves our cautious respect and understanding but not our intellectual agreement. The trouble with the African's prescientific attitude is that it lacks sufficiently critical assessment of tradition, custom, and habitual ways of ordering the world. If hunger could be eliminated by human imaginative efforts, including the development of an appropriate technology, then the tradition that blindly clings to preserving the order of things must be rejected on the behalf of critical humanism and common sense. The will to conserve habits that destroy well-being and dignity is unreasonable and stupid. The meditative individuals in Africa should subject the prescientific attitude to critical scrutiny in terms of an intelligent and modest appropriation of scientific progress in Africa. Hountondji deserves our respect when he challenges the African individual to develop a scientific cast of mind.[1] Science should not be wholeheartedly condemned. African pride must give way to intelligence and imagination.

In the quest of developing Africa, African philosophy can play a major role. The question of the existence or nonexistence of African philosophy is moot. To ask if there is an African philosophy is to ask indirectly if there are human beings in Africa who think. At the minimum, philosophy demands thinking or meditating; the Ethiopian Zara Yaquob is a genuine meditator, as are many other Africans. African individuals' mode of philosophizing is born both from struggle and from wonder of the design of the universe. They think about the nature of the god who has condemned them to suffer, and in this way participate in metaphysical thinking. When they fail to enjoy life, they wonder why. They do not write down their thoughts. Nonetheless, they are potential writers. Kundera said the following:

> every individual without exception bears a potential
> writer within himself and . . . all mankind has every

---

[1]Hountondji, *African Philosophy* (Bloomington: Indiana University Press, 1983).

right to rush out into the streets with a cry of "we are all writers!"[2]

Philosophy is useful not only as systematic and metanarrative but also as a moral activity. As a moral activity philosophy can draw rather heavily from the other aspect of life-world, the life-world as the home of care, compassion, cooperation, and a deep respect for external nature. The traditional African life-world does not serve the African peasant when it prevents all that needs radical change in his way of life. Refusal to cut the trees so as to feed the hungry is foolish and destructive. There is truth to the proposition that God helps those who help themselves. When the African peasant clings to worn-out myths, he plants the seeds of his destruction; no one—God included—will help him. Only the detractors of the African peasant encourage the African peasant to refuse to use his intelligence to bring about material development.

The intimidating presence of nature makes it necessary for African farmers to break the distance of their individualities. The tendency to be at each other's throats, the desire to use power to dominate each other is considerably controlled by nature against which they collectively must defend themselves. It is the fear of external nature that draws the African individual peasants together to care for each other's well-being. The fear of nature produces the proclivity to develop morally sensitive ways of living.

In the traditional African life-world technocratic backwardness and the resistance to modernization is balanced by moral richness and charity. Modernity needs to revitalize the moral richness of the prereflective stages of the life-world. Whereas the African peasant's resistance to science as a whole may be criticized, his moral sentiments are admirable, so admirable that they can serve as the foundation of African philosophy.

To say that the self's disposition in the life-world of the African farmer is morally rich is to say that the reflective and comprehensively reasonable way of life is practiced with ease. It is precisely such a disposition that makes it possible for philosophy to draw out some guiding principles from human beings. As

---

[2]Kundera, *The Book of Laughter and Forgetting* (New York: Penguin Books, 1987), 106.

175

reflective and reasonable beings, we may assume the African farmers to be guided by self-generated internal principles which make them control their impulses to produce wealth and luxury for themselves.

If the African food crisis is to be overcome, the power holders in Africa and their counterparts abroad must agree to develop working principles. These principles can be inserted into a continentally applicable constitution. To function as solid tools of public policy, these principles must become laws. Once the principles are formally structured and a constitution is written, there would remain the matter of educating the African populace to internalize the duties of substantial membership in a pan-African community. This ideal will take time. Furthermore, the corrupt elements of the continent must be punished if and when they transgress the dictates of the constitution.

Chapter 5 enunciated the following two principles which should lead the discourse of public policy amidst the development of Africa: alleviation of the food crisis, and the preparation of the continent for modernization with a moral vision—a vision that may result in the construction of an African ethical community.

The two principles are:

The first principle is the recognition of food, health, shelter, and clothing as inalienable human rights. African resources must be used in such a way that they can, with proper scientific aids, be channelled to eventually (a) eliminate the urgent human needs of poverty and hunger, and (b) address other attendant consequences of mental and physical health, hopelessness, and undermotivation.

The second principle is a demand for the absolutely necessary duty humans may have in the recognition of the importance of freedom for those who think and feel that they are unfree. When the basic human material needs of the poor are met, only then may the Africans be able to think about nonmaterial human needs, such as art and religion.

Human beings capable of sympathizing with their fellows are endowed with a capacity for justice. Sometimes they behave as if they did not have this capacity and we see them hurting and

176

resenting others. The presence of justice requires that we distance ourselves from the things immediately important to us; it requires putting ourselves in the condition of pure thoughtfulness, a kind of coolness. Then justice comes to our service, to enable us to engage in an "expanded horizon" of the aspiration of others. It is the power of our unsocial and selfish passions which makes it difficult for our sense of justice to regulate our everyday life.

If given their sense of justice, if people reflect upon the harmful consequences of their thoughtless and impulsive actions, they might begin to see the unworthiness of their actions and their odious inhumanness. When such actions are subjected to analysis, their unworthiness becomes self-evident, moral shame overcomes the doer. Help for people in Africa who need material help, if performed with the proper mental attitude, could result in African peasants becoming self-reliant, and those who help become rationally and morally complete human beings.

We must emphasize the need for educating people to live a rational moral life in a democratic community. Education is a crucial dimension of any theory of morality and political economy; much less crucial is the role of the educator except as a guide whose help may be solicited by the members of a community. In a future ethical community, education toward the reflective rational moral life will be much more important than the discovery, disclosure, or explication of the implicit moral powers of humankind. Of course, our conscience can work along with the potentiality of our consciousness such that the end of education might be the possibility of habitually engaging our consciences to help us decide, to enable us to embark upon the path of doing the right thing, and to undertake the morally right action.

If it were possible to legislate for humankind the morally right road to pursue, or the path of justice to follow, and if humankind had the capacity to translate the legislation into praxis, then humankind would have solved its perennial problem: the task of ethics to guide action. Most human beings, however, have neither found the ethical community nor shown an inclination to think and act morally. The "unexamined life" as Socrates called it, or the irresponsible, indifferent, amoral life is often treated in the educational sphere as the natural dimension of the human condition. The task of moral philosophy in a period of moral indifference then is first to found an argument that conceives of men and women not only as economic beings but as moral/rational beings.

A popular, scientific, and unusual culture as well as political and moral awareness are the pillars upon which the creation of an African community can be grounded. The foundation is an ethical community guided by self-generated principles and aiming at the eventual diffusion of a continental perspective. The continental perspective may enable Africans to look at themselves as the members of a continent with many resources, capable of overcoming the problems to which the two principles refer. The first principle requires science, appropriate technology, and agricultural machinery which African farmers may use.

INDEX

179